Experience the Wonder in You

Experience the wonder in you . . . and the magic you can create.

Author: Karen van Huizen

All rights reserved. No part of this publication may be reproduced, stored in a retrieval system or transmitted in any form by any means, electronic or mechanical, including photocopying and recording, without the prior written permission of the author. Enquiries should be made to the publisher.

Published by: van Huizen Design
ABN: 18 542 017 065
experiencethewonder@vanhdesign.com.au

Copyright 2010   Karen van Huizen

Every effort has been made to ensure that this book is free from error or omissions. However, the Publisher, the Author or their respective employees or agents, shall not accept responsibility for injury, loss or damage occasioned to any person acting or refraining from action as a result of material in this book whether or not such injury, loss or damage is in any way due to negligent act or omission, breach of duty or default on the part of the Publisher, the Author, or their respective employees or agents.

National Library of Australia
Title: Experience the Wonder in You
ISBN 978-0-9808335-0-8

Cover Design: Bulldog Creatrix   **www.bulldogcreatrix.com.au**
Photo: Fran O'Connor - Studio 3   **www.studio3melbourne.com.au**

Edition: 1
Printed By: Tingleman   **www.tingleman.com.au**

To order additional copies of this book visit
    Web: www.vanhdesign.com.au
                www.thedirectionofdreams.com
    Email: experiencethewonder@vanhdesign.com.au

Experience the
Wonder in You

and the magic you can create

A journey of self discovery and creation

Karen van Huizen

About the Author

My married name is Karen van Huizen. My life has not been one of particular hardship, but a life that I am sure most of you can relate to. My journey has assisted me in becoming the person I am today, and my life experiences have helped to shape the decisions I have made in order to bring me to this point where I can now be an influential stand for others, so that you may also learn to "create magic in your life".

I am the eldest Child of three, each of us born in a different state of Australia for, in my younger years, my father was in the Royal Australian Air Force, and we moved a lot, in fact 17 times by the time I was 22 years old. When my father was posted overseas, I spent quite a bit of time living on the family dairy farm, and the love of the land is something that has stayed in my blood. I can not explain it in words why it is so, but the wide open spaces calm and inspire me.

My youngest sister, 6 years my junior, has special needs. I did not find this to be a problem because I

About the Author

did not know any different. She was my sister, and I loved her. Later in life, I came to realise how much she has to rely on outside help and us for her every need, however, she seems to be happy, and that is all that matters.

I grew up with asthma and bronchitis, and began swimming to help strengthen my lungs. I joined a swimming and lifesaving club and enjoyed competing until the age of 17, when I broke my right foot and injured my back in a horse riding accident. Fortunately, after nearly 6 months in plaster and surgery on my foot, I made a full recovery.

Although I gave up the competition in the pool, I continued on the beaches and took up teaching swimming and lifesaving. I enjoyed having the opportunity to be of service to people as I loved being able to pass on my knowledge by teaching others to do the same. It was then that I was awarded the "Certificate of Thanks" from the Royal Lifesaving Society on behalf of the Queen, for services rendered to the Society. This was a big honour, and I cherish it.

At College I studied Architectural Drafting and

About the Author

went on to study Interior Design. It was in drafting class that I met my husband Paul. Before we were married, we decided to build our home. It took 2 $^1/_2$ years of working evenings and weekends, with the help of family and friends, to finally achieve our dream of building our ideal mud brick home.

Our aim was to be as "green" as we possibly could. Our approach was to make every space practical and usable whilst being aesthetically pleasing. The build was a challenge to our Bodies and to our Minds as we did most of the physical work ourselves, but by golly, it was worthwhile.

Because of my Asthma, Paul suffering from what they thought was Chronic Fatigue, Paul's Mum passing away from Cancer and our first son Matthew showing early signs of Asthma at 18 months, I went looking for answers to our health challenges.

After a long search, I was introduced to a company which produced personal care products and nutritional supplements without using potentially harmful ingredients. We switched brands and began taking their supplements to repair and support our bodies.

About the Author

I researched thoroughly the products and how they could help our bodies, and passed on the information I had gained, so that I could help others achieve the results I had. Asthma became a thing of the past, and Paul's Chronic Fatigue went. I was so impressed by my results that I began distributing for this company, and I hit one of the highest ranks you can achieve. To this day, my family and I continue to use and enjoy the benefits of their products as well as the remuneration.

Just like with the lifesaving, I enjoyed helping people by showing them how to help themselves and other people . . . and other people . . . a theme began to show in my life.

Just before having our second son Joel, I was suffering with depression. At that point, I made the commitment that my life was to be one of example to our children, not "a warning". I took up personal development in a big way.

As I learnt new life changing strategies, I began sharing them with others so that they could achieve the positive results I was getting. Again, I loved the opportunity to support others around me.

About the Author

I have since studied Permaculture (living sustainably). I have always wanted to make a difference with people and the planet, and living my life by example is the best way to do so.

Over the years I have learned a lot and continue to learn a little bit more every day. Someone once said to me "Never go to bed not having learned something new today". That was good advice. I am continually inspired by the people that I get to work with, and those who are so generous with their knowledge.

Nowadays, my life is abundant and fulfilling, and I thank you for the privilege of being able to share some of myself with you. I hope that you can take the information within these pages and use it to create your own success story.

The possibilities are infinite.

Now let's begin with you . . .

Contents

Introduction		1
Suggested Use		5
Chapter 1	How does this Journey begin?	11

Part 1 – The Wonder of Me

Chapter 2	Who or What is in Control of Me?	19
Chapter 3	My Body	27
Chapter 4	My Mind	37
Chapter 5	My Soul	51

Part 2 – Working with Me

Chapter 6	My Personality	61
Chapter 7	It's Okay to be Me	73
Chapter 8	My Feelings	81
Chapter 9	My Choices	91

Chapter 10	My Beliefs	103
Chapter 11	My Past	115
Chapter 12	Where am I now?	123
Chapter 13	What am I expecting?	131
Chapter 14	What am I attracting?	139

Part 3 – Nurturing Me

Chapter 15	My Time	157
Chapter 16	Nurturing my Body	167
Chapter 17	Nurturing my Mind	175
Chapter 18	Nurturing my Soul	181

Part 4 – Creating Magic

Chapter 19	Where am I going?	189
Chapter 20	My Plan	199
Chapter 21	Regrouping Diary	217

| Chapter 22 | Me Sharing | 229 |
| Chapter 23 | My Patience | 239 |

Part 5 – The Beginning

Chapter 24	The Beginning	253
Final Note		259
Dedication		261

Introduction

Grab a comfy seat and let's get a little more acquainted before we begin this journey together. I have written this book especially for you. Enjoy experiencing the wonder of you and the magic that you truly can create.

I have decided to place my dedication and thanks at the end of the book for two reasons. Firstly I want to get right to the book and secondly because the end is really the beginning.

Your reasons may be varied for picking up this book. It may be that you want to change the state of a relationship, have better results in your job or your finances. You may want to feel more fulfilled and happy in your life or you may even just be curious to see what others are talking about. No matter what your reason is for picking up the book, what I am going to share with you can help in all areas of your life.

It started for me after spending many years fighting off depression. Don't get me wrong I had a good life, well some of it may not have been so good, but on the whole I had nothing I could complain about. I didn't even know where the depression came from. I began to notice how many people around me were struggling too. I decided my life had to be different.

Introduction

I did not want to go to a psychiatrist, psychologist or therapist who could tell me all of the things that were wrong with me. I did not want to find someone or something to blame, I just wanted to find out how to be happy and flow with the changes as they happened in my life. Actually, I wanted to create change; positive change in my life. Rather than look at the problem I decided to search for the solution.

I made a choice. Rather than medicate myself to numb my feelings I was going to face those feelings head on, search for answers and create a life and a world in which I am truly happy, balanced and fulfilled.

I decided to take responsibility for my thoughts, feelings and actions and create different results in my life. Little was I to know that I would find me; it all came down to *Me*. I could make a difference in my life. I began to enjoy learning about *Me* and how I could change things if I really wanted to.

I read many books, listened to many tapes and CDs, watched DVDs and attended programs on personal development. I continue to learn on a daily basis and I believe it is a life long journey that will only end when I draw my last breath.

I have used all that I have learnt to date to put the pieces of the puzzle that was my life together. I have found that the solutions are never as hard as I first thought.

Introduction

My life is now filled with happiness and optimism. Of course, there is the odd day when I don't feel myself, however, the downs are not like the depressed feelings I used to have, besides, how would I know a good day if I didn't have an average one every now and again.

I have taken all that I have learnt and put it in this book so that you can benefit from what I have learnt.

I will share with you some of my experiences throughout the book. I do ask that you open your mind and allow me to take you on a journey so that you may find the good that you are seeking in your own life.

I believe most of it comes down to understanding and taking responsibility for *Me* in all that I do, and continuing to improve myself each and every day. Do I always get it right? No, but I learn from each day. I choose carefully what I think and what I want in my life, but most importantly I am grateful for every experience and all that I have in my life.

You see, there was nothing wrong with me in the first place. It was as simple as getting to know myself. I am where I am, doing the best that I can with what I know. That doesn't mean that is where I have to stay tomorrow as I know I have choices.

The question is where do *You* go from here? Take the time to read on and I will give you the tools to come to

Introduction

know and understand *You* and how to create the life *You* truly desire.

I encourage you to take your own journey head on. Enjoy discovering and creating the life that *You* deserve to have.

Suggested Use

As you read this book, it may be easy to say "I know that" or "It's just common sense". You may also have heard some of this information before explained in a different way. If you catch yourself saying or thinking this it may be a good time to ask yourself the question;

‍*I* may know this, but am *I* applying it to *my* life and getting the results I want?

It may be worth taking some time to practice making small changes and monitor the results that you get. Rather than looking for a big "Ah Ha" (realisation) or the "magic bullet" I have found that it's more about fine tuning what I do. One small change of habit may make the difference and give you the result that you want.

You can choose to go through the book slowly doing all of the exercises. Alternatively I suggest you read the book right through to the end and then come back to the beginning to go through it slowly. You will pick up more the second time around. When you go back through do all of the exercises, you may be surprised at what you find out about yourself. As you read, ask yourself **"how can *I* apply this to *my* life?"**

You may want to ask a family member, friend or business associate if they'd like to work through the book with you. Decide to read a chapter at a time or choose a number of pages you both agree to, and make a time to discuss and analyse what you read, and then tell each other what changes you want to implement in your life. This way you can support each other. Keeping a diary may be helpful in this process.

When you are doing this it is important to remember that no two people are alike. Even twins have a different thumb print. Your past experiences and how you interpret them will be vastly different from anyone else's. What you learn in a particular chapter may be different from the person that you are sharing the journey with, however, what you learn may help them to see something else in themselves which may move them forwards and vice versa.

If you don't have someone to share your journey with at the moment stay connected through: www.thedirectionofdreams.com You can read other people's comments and share your own success story through the blog or ask a question via the contact page.

Practice makes Improvement

A great analogy to describe the process of "improving" is a story I have learnt about a pothole in the road. A man travelled down the road and fell into a pothole, got stuck and had to figure how to get out. The next day he fell into the pothole again but knew how to get out quickly. A few days later he was able to see the pothole coming and swerved to miss it. A week or so later he got to the street and remembered the pothole and took another street. A month later the man was daydreaming and headed down the street accidentally. He remembered the pothole and quickly swerved to avoid it and thought to himself "I should pay more attention to what I am doing".

This is such a great analogy to understanding that you don't have to get it all together right away. It is a process. Enjoy the journey and remember to acknowledge yourself for the little achievements along the way. Sometimes it may look as if you have taken a step backwards when you go down the road with the pothole. See it as confirmation that you really have learnt the lesson.

Progress in the lesson can be broken down into 3 phases.

Suggested Use

Phase 1 – The Blind Spot.

Sometimes I find myself in a situation that I don't really want to be in, again, doing the same thing with the same people in similar circumstances. I sometimes recognise it after the event and how it made me feel. I have absolutely no power at that stage to choose a different outcome.

Phase 2 – Observation.

I find myself in a situation that I don't really want to be in anymore, doing the same thing with the same people in similar circumstances. In the middle of the "event" I realise I'm here again and can see how I "set it all up" to be this way. It is like I become the observer of the situation. Identifying the problem helps me to make choices in the future.

Phase 3 – Choice.

I observe myself "setting up the situation" that I don't want to be in anymore, doing the same thing with the same people in similar circumstances and I choose not to have that experience again. I kindly and lovingly say "I'm not available to do that on that day" or words to that effect. I feel good because I have stood in my power and that is progress!

If you continue to
do what you have
always done,
you will continue
to get what
you have always got.

– Socrates

Chapter 1

How does this Journey begin?

How does this Journey begin?

As I said in the Introduction, this book has been put together using all of the material and personal experiences that I have had or witnessed to date that have worked. It is set out in simple terms using examples and exercises to help you grasp the concepts. You can also stay connected through my website at www.thedirectionofdreams.com so that you can learn from the success of others and share your own success stories

My aim is to take you on a journey of self discovery. To give you a step by step process to understanding yourself and how you can positively work with change in your life. As I said, the information is simple and the exercises can be fun, however, the results that you will achieve from reading and doing the exercises can be beyond your wildest dreams. Some of the exercises may seem simple and insignificant, but if you choose to make the changes in your life to move you in the direction of your dreams, do the exercises, and put what you learn into action, the results will come.

I spoke about how I suffered depression in my Introduction and how I did not want to medicate myself. I just want to make one thing clear before I go any further. There are many causes of depression and I do not suggest that you throw away your medication. I had to balance my hormones and that made a big difference. I began to supplement with vitamins and minerals to look after my body. If you follow the book and complete the exercises you may find that you no longer require your medication in which case you can do this with the support of a practitioner.

We begin with an understanding of how our thoughts, feelings and actions create results in our life. By having an understanding of how something works then it is easier to make changes. Then we will put together a picture of what really makes you who you are and explore the hidden talents that make you unique. You will understand why it is okay to be you no matter what anyone says, and with continued growth you can let your unique talents emerge, grow and radiate.

We will then look at your life up to now and show you how with continued growth you can change outcomes in your life. I will show you how to achieve your goals and learn to dream. I will give you some steps that you can put into place to work with that will nurture the Body, Mind & Soul. You will find that achieving your goals, happiness and balance can be fun and rewarding.

I have said that I have used all of the techniques that I am sharing with exceptional results. I also realise through experience that it is not only easy to do; it is also easy not to do. Just like going to the gym it is all about choice and taking responsibility for having an exceptional life. There may be some short term pain but the long term gain is definitely worth it.

My wish is for you to take this information with the knowledge that whatever you can conceive, you can achieve. This book will give you the knowledge to have the faith in yourself to make clear choices which will help you to achieve whatever you desire.

You don't have to see the whole staircase; just that first step.

- Martin Luther King Jr.

Part 1
The Wonder of Me

Chapter 2

Who or What is in Control of Me?

Who or What is in Control of Me?

"*I* am in control of *me*."
"*I* am in control of all *I* do,
the results *I* get and
the life *I* have."

I am responsible for
my thoughts, *my* feelings
my actions and all
the results *I* have in *my* life.

This is a big statement. Take some time to think about it. What do I mean when I say "Me"? In fact what makes you?

How can I be expected to be responsible for my results if I don't understand where they come from? How can I change my actions so that I can change my results? How can I possibly be responsible for controlling my thoughts and my feelings if I don't even know where they come from?

Who or What is in Control of Me?

To begin, I am going to give you a brief explanation of what I mean by thoughts, feelings and actions, and how they create the results in our life. Then we will start your journey of self discovery with an understanding of who you are. This will help you to work with the thoughts, feelings and actions you need to get the results that you are looking for in your life.

When we have a thought there is usually a feeling that is connected to that thought. The feelings may range from empowering thoughts such as happiness, excitement, contentment and the list goes on. They may also be dis-empowering thoughts such as fear, jealousy, anger and the list also goes on. Think about how people act when they are excited for a moment. They may jump up and down, have a smile on their face and talk quite quickly. Now think about how a person may act if they are angry. They may yell, pace and rant and rave in a very loud voice.

I say my thoughts, my feelings and my actions because they usually come in that particular order. It would be fair to say that the results that we have in our life are usually a result of the actions that we take.
To make permanent changes it is best to start at the beginning of the process. Since our emotions are a result of our thoughts wouldn't it make sense to change the thought process first?

Who or What is in Control of Me?

Why do we have thoughts?

Where do they come from?

How do we change them?

Until you can answer these questions, it may be a little difficult to make changes to your thoughts. To get the results that you want it would be wise to get a clear understanding of "self". More importantly what makes you who you are?

There are three parts to you that make you unique. These parts are not separate, one part can not exist without the other and they connect to each other like the colors of the rainbow. These three parts interweave to make the whole. You may have heard each part spoken about before. They have been described in various different ways.

1. **Body** everyone can identify with the Body as they can physically see it

2. **Mind** often referred to as the conscious Mind or your head

3. **Soul** often referred to as the sub-conscious Mind or your heart

Before you make any judgment about the fact that you have a Body, Mind and Soul; take the time to read on and sit with the idea until I paint you a picture. The picture is to ensure we are both "working" with the same image when I explain the Body, Mind and Soul.

We are a river of intelligence, information and energy that is in an ever constant exchange with the rest of the huge reservoir of intelligence, information and energy.

- Deepak Chopra

Chapter 3

My Body

My Body

The Body is the most recognised part about Man. The Body is the physical part of us. It is the part that we can physically see. I said that I would give you a picture of the Body, Mind and Soul. I will use the stick figure drawing for the Body as it is recognised by everyone.

Now that we have a picture for the Body, the next step is to make sure that you have a clear understanding of what the Body is, and is not. Then we will look at the Body in relation to the Mind.

Our Body is a magnificent instrument. It runs like a

machine and has many functions that go on within it, without our conscious awareness. I am not going to give you an anatomy lesson here. If you want to know more about how the Body works there are plenty of reference books on the subject. Science has studied the Body over many centuries and they still can not fully understand how it performs. One reference that I have found to be very good is the books and CDs by Deepak Chopra who is a medical doctor and also a spiritual healer. He explains the Body simply in both a physical and spiritual sense.

What I find amazing is the fact that we have a totally new Body approximately every 2 years. We have new bones every 90 days, new skin every 30 days, a new stomach lining every 5 days and new taste buds every 6 weeks. Over the course of 2 years every cell in our Body has been replaced, including our brain cells.

If I ask someone to picture the Mind, quite often they have a picture of the brain. The brain is not the Mind, if it was scientists would have the brains of Albert Einstein and all of the other great Minds in history bottled in laboratories and they would be finding ways to use or study their Minds right now.

The Brain is a part of the Body which is used by the Body and the Mind. If it was not connected to the Mind, how else would my new taste buds know that I love the taste of mango, cherries, cheese or chocolate? If I have a totally new Body every 2 years, even though I have not played with a yo-yo for many years how would my new Body still know how to play a yo-yo?

The brain has many functions. It controls the biological processes within the Body, takes information from the senses of the Body and records it. It will also send chemicals around the Body in response to stimuli.

The main function of the Body is movement. The Body moves, speaks, acts or reacts in certain ways with the use of the brain depending on the information that is fed to it from the Mind. That is what we mean by the action that gets the results in our life.

The Body has physical senses; the main 5 that science has defined are taste, touch, sight, smell and sound. We use these senses to gather information around us. In fact scientists have argued that there are up to 22 senses. They include your sense of humor and sense of time, balance and direction. Touch can be broken into a number of senses in itself. With touch you have a sense of pressure and this could be related to how heavy something is, there is the sense of pain and the sense of heat where we can tell how hot or cold something is. Let's keep it simple and stick to the basics with one inclusion.
Most people have heard of the kinesthetic sense. I believe that this is an important sense that we have which is attached to the unseen part of us. This is how

you can close your eyes and still be able to find your nose with your finger, it is how you can pass a ball behind your back without looking at it and it is also how you can "feel" when someone is walking behind you when you haven't seen them yet.

This is part of our connection to everything else in the cosmos. When spiritualists say that we are connected to everything it is not something that you can see with the naked eye. But when we take it back to basics in a physical sense we are always connected to something.

Take the time to think about it. If you are sitting right now you are connected to the chair and maybe even the floor. If you are not touching the floor you are connected anyway as the chair is connected to the floor. You are connected to your clothes, this book and maybe even some jewellery. Some of your jewellery may not just be connected; piercing actually passes through your Body. Cool huh?

So, if I am connected to the floor and so are you then we are connected to each other. In fact there is a method of photography called Curlean photography that photographs the energy or cells as they leave the Body. The rate and density of light or energy can change due to your state of Mind. You may call it a mood or feeling. A person in a depressed state shows as a darker colour and more dense which does not radiate far from the Body. Someone in a happy state of Mind is shown as a lighter colour and radiates out further from the Body.

Using our kinesthetic sense we feel energy leaving a Body. (It has also been referred to as an aura.) This is why you can feel tension in a room when you walk in, you don't even need to see the person's face and they do not even have to utter a word and you can automatically "read" what is going on. Alternatively you may also feel drawn to someone who radiates a "good" or "light" energy.

Some people who are born without or lose one of the 5 senses usually have a heightened awareness in another sense to compensate for the loss. You can see this with someone who is blind. Their kinesthetic sense or their sense of hearing is usually more acute. You might say they are more "Tuned In" to that sense. I will explain more about how we Tune In later in the chapter "What am I attracting".

If you are looking at a flower you would use your senses to identify it by its shape, colour, size, fragrance and a number of other features including the name that you were given for that particular flower. The collected data is stored in the Brain. The Brain also stores your feelings towards the flower. This information is accessed by the Mind at any given time.

Isn't the Body an amazing thing? Understanding helps me to appreciate each part of the Body in the overall big picture of what makes me who I am and my connection to everything else. Take the time to think about the Body and how fascinating its mechanisms are, even if we don't understand them they are still working. Understanding helps us to work powerfully with the Body.

Take care of your Body. It's the only place you have to live.

- Jim Rohn

Chapter 4

My Mind

My Mind

In the previous chapter called My Body, I discussed the fact that the Mind is not the brain. The brain produces electrical signals together with chemical reactions to let parts of the Body communicate. Nerves send these signals throughout the Body. The Mind and the Body utilise the brain to power you. The Mind is connected to the Body like the colors of the rainbow are connected. We could say that the Body is within the Mind. To give you a clear concept of what I have just said I will add to our simple stick figure of the Body a picture of what represents the Mind.

I know sometimes it's not easy to grasp what we can not see physically but understanding helps us to grasp the concept and form a picture. A great example is when a stone is tossed into a Body of water.

If you throw a stone into a puddle you can physically see the water move and change. If you throw a stone into the ocean you create the same sort of changes, in fact, you change the whole shoreline. You may not be able to physically see it but with understanding you can create a picture in your Mind of what happens to the ocean when you throw in the stone.

Now that I have given you a picture to represent the Mind let's explore what the Mind is.

The Mind has two functions.

1. ***The Conscious Mind*** which is the intellectual part of our nature. It is the part of us that reasons, exercises free will, works with logic and sets goals.

2. ***The Sub-conscious Mind*** which works with the feeling part of our nature. It builds habits and beliefs based on the emotions that we have. This is the part of the Mind that will help you to achieve your goals.

    It is responsible for instructing the Brain to send the electrical signals and chemicals to the Body in response to the information that it has. This is what gives the feelings to the Body in response to the information that it receives.

My Mind

The Conscious and Sub-conscious Mind are symbolised as your head and your heart. One is logical and the other is emotional. The Soul is not symbolised as the heart.

The basic function of the Mind is to collect, store and retrieve data utilising the Body which houses the Brain. It is the part of us that does the questioning. It will look for data from our past to see if it can find a match, then it "warns" us about all the things that may go "wrong". Have you ever had a great idea and then started to question and doubt yourself. The doubt is the Mind questioning.

Your Mind is a marvelous part of you. If you understand how the two parts of your Mind function then you will be able to work with it and nurture it powerfully. We have already discussed that it is working anyway so you may as well make it work for you rather than against you.

Let's explore how the Mind works in more depth.

If you are old enough you may remember when you were learning to drive a car, Your Mind probably flashed a little movie through the screen in your Mind the minute I asked you to remember it. They may be good memories or not so good memories.
You may have stalled many times, done "bunny hops" and I'm sure probably crunched a few gears. At first

your Mind was given all the information that you needed. The Mind then had to work with the Brain to help your Body work with that information to move your hands and feet at the right time to get the result of driving the car. You would have built neural pathways doing this over and over until a "habit or belief" had been formed between the Mind and the Body. You would have practiced driving in the rain and hill starts. All of these functions may have required different knowledge and movements. These days you don't think about the clutch and the gears. You probably just hop in the car and drive. Even if the cells change in your Body the memory in the Mind programs the cells to be able to continue to drive the car even if you are not consciously thinking about driving the car.

You may have had an occasion when you wanted to drop off somewhere on the way home and all of a sudden noticed that you were almost home. You were probably "somewhere else" thinking about something when suddenly you realised what you were doing. Now who was driving the car? The Mind would have looked for the piece of information that it required to keep you going as it knew you were driving, but it picked up the habit you had formed of going home that way and continued on. Humm, I think we've all done that at least once.

You may have even had an experience where you noticed in time to make the turn to where you were going or avoid a potential accident. This is where your Soul would have given you the inspiration to pay attention and then be able to get your Mind back on track.

I am about to explain something important. This may help you understand why things may happen to you the way that they do, but may not happen for someone else. If your Mind is wondering at this point, I suggest that you take a break and come back when you are fresh to receive what I am about to tell you.

Are you feeling fresh? Great! Now let's get down to it.

When something happens in your life (I call it an "event") your Sub-conscious Mind will cause your Body to react or respond in a certain way within a split second.

What your Mind will do is act like a big filing cabinet and look through the data from all the events that have happened to you to date and try to match it to something. The Mind may even take that data and if it finds anything there that it thinks may be harmful to you it will warn you usually in the form of a feeling (The Brain will send an electrical signal or a set of chemicals around the Body to give the Body the feeling that is matched with the thought). This will put the Body into action. It may not always be the reaction you wanted.

My Mind

The Body can become addicted to these electrical signals or chemicals. The feeling that you have may become what you perceive to be your identity. It is what you believe yourself to be when you feel that way.

Quite often the event that is happening before your eyes is not the same scenario as the data that is retrieved. This gives a distorted view of what is actually happening. Just like the driving of the car.

It could be information about something that was said, heard, felt or experienced by you in the past. It might be similar but it is not the same. Then what can happen is the new data gets added to the old data and forms a bigger piece of data that may then be retrieved in the future if another similar "event" arises.

Do you see how a distorted view on the "event" can occur? Someone may have yelled at you and hit you for doing something "wrong" when you were young. When someone yells at you in the present, you may feel "you didn't get it right" which may result in an awful feeling. This feeling may even be fear. The Mind is probably in the back ground saying "be careful, you may get hit" or your Mind will work with the brain which will send a chemical response around the Body which may give you the feeling of fear and cause your Body to move backwards for protection. Now, if it is your teacher or boss; I don't think that they are going to really hit you are they? That is what I mean by a distorted view. You do things even though they don't make sense to you. You may even walk away thinking "Why did I do that?"

When a mother smiles a lot at her baby the neurological pathways are formed and depending on the other information that the baby takes in from its other senses at the same time it forms a belief, habit or memory about the smile. Usually when Mum is smiling at the baby she is saying something nice to the baby in a nice tone of voice. The baby's Mind would then store the smile as a good feeling and begin associating smiling with happiness.

Let's say the baby was constantly smiled at only briefly as the mother passed the baby and was muttering in an angry voice. It is possible that the baby could form a different set of thoughts and feelings associated with a smile. Would you agree that the thoughts and feelings that the baby may have associated with a smile could cause mixed thoughts and emotions later in life when people smiled at him if he did not change the thought and feeling associated with a smile to one that we recognise to be happy and joyful.

We form beliefs and habits from all of the information that the Mind collects. If you were to grow up seeing no love shown between your parents in a marriage how would you know anything else? Unless you gather other information from being around couples with loving marriages, seeing love shown or reading about loving relationships you wouldn't know how to have a loving marriage. The Mind is responsible for containing all of this information.

Now some would say that a loveless marriage is not a good thing. I believe that we make up what are good and bad in our Mind depending on our experience. One person may think that a passionate kiss is good and another may be repulsed by it depending on the thoughts and feelings stored in their Mind. There is no right and wrong. A problem will only arise if the person sees that there is a problem with it.

In some situations the problem may arise when a society deems that it is wrong. In Australia we have laws which do not allow you to "beat" your wife. In a few countries it is part of the culture to "beat" your wife and is quite accepted. I am not passing any judgment on this scenario; however, any man arriving in Australia from a culture that allows "beating" may have problems or be judged for his behavior. He may have grown up believing that it is the thing to do but he may have to change his belief if he is to live in Australia.

The great thing about the Mind is that we can change how we think and feel about something "by choice". By continuing to make a choice we can change the habit or belief. This is why I believe that having a clear understanding of how the Mind works, you can learn strategies to enable you to "Change your Mind," and how you feel about certain things, at will.

I like to picture the Mind like a little puppy. It is innocent and takes in everything that is around it. You need to train the puppy so that it knows how to behave otherwise you could have a puppy that grows into a very naughty dog. You have to train your Mind just like you train a puppy. It doesn't know if what you put in there is good or bad, it is just information that it retrieves in the form of habits, beliefs and memories. It is wise to be firm with a puppy, give it lots of praise and encouragement and focus on what it does right or well. It is not nice to beat the puppy if it does something wrong. It is better to let it know when it has bad behavior and concentrate on praising it for the things it does well. This method will result in a happy, well adjusted dog. If you want a healthy Mind it is wise to do the same.

I gave an explanation in the chapter on Suggested Use of this book about 3 phases of growth or progress. The first is identifying the belief or habit (your blind spot). The second was observing it and the third is having the choice to change it when you see it. If you are committed to continual growth, you will be open to see the "blind spots," and the techniques that I give you on your journey through this book, will support you to work with that change. One thing that will help you to work with change is your Soul. Before you move on to learning about the Soul take the time to recognise how powerful your Mind can be. When you learn to work with your Mind you can create some very powerful beliefs which will help you to create some amazing results in your life.

You can teach an old dog new tricks - it just has to want to.

- Karen van Huizen

Chapter 5

My Soul

My Soul

The word "Soul" conjures up many varied thoughts and feelings for people. At the beginning of this book I asked that you be open. If the word "Soul" holds certain beliefs for you then I ask that you stay receptive while I give you some further information so that you can make an informed decision.

After reading this chapter you may find that the belief you have about the Soul is strengthened by my explanation or you may find that your belief no longer serves you, in which case you have the choice to change it if you wish.

The Soul has been called a number of things, heart, spirit, essence etc. It is often referred to as spirit. Like the Mind, it is a part of you that is unseen by the naked eye. I said that the Body is within the Mind. The Soul is not separate from you. The Body, Mind and Soul connect with each other to become one like the colours of the rainbow. To give you a picture to represent the Soul I will again add to the stick figure drawing.

The Soul is neither good, nor bad, it just is. It can't be bought and it can't be sold. The Soul is the part of you that works with your feeling nature. Not with touch, but your feelings. It is the part of you that gives you insights. It is the part that is in touch with what Man does not fully understand, even though it is studied in many forms from religion to science through quantum physics. It is the part of us that connects us to nature, the earth, the cosmos and all that is around us. The "All Mighty".

I said the "All Mighty" because you know for yourself what you know to be true. I am not going to challenge any beliefs in this book with regard to any religion. The information that I am presenting here is an explanation of the Body, Mind & Soul which connects us to everything including the "All Mighty".

I hope that you can be open enough to understand that I respect everyone's own beliefs, just as I expect to be respected for mine.

My Soul

The Soul is in touch with everything. We are connected to everything on a physical and spiritual vibration. The difference is the vibration.

Everything in this universe vibrates at different frequencies and speeds. They rub up against each other. Water comprises of two parts hydrogen and one part oxygen which vibrate together to give us what we call water. You can change the vibration of those molecules by freezing them and they become ice. Change them again with heat and they become steam, continue to heat them and they become air, ether or gas. At that vibration we can not see them but they are still there vibrating on a different level. Just because something can not be seen, doesn't mean that it does not exist.

In the chapter My Body I discussed how we are connected to everything and how we can even feel peoples' mood. You could also call it their state of vibration. If the Soul rubs up against another Soul it can feel their vibration through the senses.

Are we Souls living in a physical Body or are we Souls who have a physical Body? Either way we are Souls having a physical experience and we are gifted with an intellect which we call the Mind.
The Soul gives us insights in the form of ideas and inspiration. It does not question and bring up negative chatter, that is the Mind speaking. The Soul is pure, simple and powers us with energy through genius and pure inspiration.

My Soul

Have you ever had that little voice in your head say "don't do that" and you questioned yourself and did it anyway, wishing afterwards that you hadn't. Well I put it to you that your Soul was giving you inspiration and your Mind questioned it and you were not listening to your Soul. You may think that "little voice" is your Mind but as I said there is your Mind and your Soul that will talk to you. One will relate it to past data and question it and the other will offer inspiration, wisdom and ideas.

So, next time when you have a great idea and someone asks you "Are you out of your Mind?" You can confidently think "Yes, I am. I am working with my Soul".

In the "My Mind" chapter I spoke about driving a car. I used the example of the Mind wandering but being able to continue driving on "automatic" so to speak. Well, I have heard of people saying that something made them look up at just the right time (for what ever reason) I believe that that was the Soul, if they needed to stop in a hurry for a red light for their safety the Soul would have inspired them to pay attention.

If you have not been exposed to this part of yourself before, you might want to try listening for that voice. Be open and read on and I will help you to explore further how to connect and work powerfully with this amazing part of yourself.

Remember the Soul will give you inspiration. If there is danger and you are connected to your Soul you will get what people call a "gut feeling". This is the difference between the Mind and the Soul.

The Mind is rational, the Soul is inspirational, and being "Tuned In" to both is extraordinary.

My Soul speaks to me with great wisdom. I listen and obey.

– Dr. De Martini

Part 2
Working with Me

Chapter 6

My Personality

My Personality

In Part 1 I discussed what makes you who you are and gave you an insight to the Body, Mind and Soul. What makes you unique is your personality; everyone is gifted with a personality. Have you ever noticed two children with the same parents yet they are so opposite in their personality, including twins? We are not all the same. Socrates originally separated people into four categories depending on the bile or phlegm that they produced. You also see a breakdown into twelve categories for personalities in the star signs. There are many ways of categorising personalities.

A part of the study into you is the understanding of your personality. This part of you is how you interpret the information that is given to you and how you reveal yourself to the outside world. This is a great piece of the puzzle to unveiling the real you.

If you study the personality types, you will find there are many books and CDs that do that. The majority of them break them down into four basic personality styles. They may call them different names or categorise them into shapes, birds or colors etc.; however, they all come down to the similar character traits. I call them gifts; they are what we were gifted with at birth. We have a little of all the gifts within us and we can develop all four gifts if we learn and apply them in our life. However, we generally operate with the two that we are most dominant in.

With each book that you read and each CD that you listen to on the different personality types you will gain added information. This will give you a deeper knowledge of yourself and others by researching the subject and having some fun with it. Each writer or speaker has a different way of presenting what they know and their personalities are also varied. I have found it fascinating to learn more about me and the people around me. It has helped me immensely in my relationships with others.

So let's have an introduction to the personalities and see if you can see yourself as a feeler, visionary, leader or entertainer. If you don't get it right away, Florence Littauer in her book "Personality Plus" says, "You could be wearing a mask". A mask is simply a gift style that you have adopted to disguise the real you for various reasons. Maybe a particular person or event has influenced your life to now. The key is to think back to how you truly were, as a child before all of your outer influences shaped you into who you are today. Give it some time to explore what gifts you feel more comfortable with then allow your true self to shine. As I said it is a process. There are many references for you to go and find out more, like Jerry Clark's CD set "The Magic of Colors". I will cover each gift briefly then, if you are interested you can seek more information to get a deeper understanding.

Each gift, like all things in life has its positive and negative side. Some gifts are stronger in some areas than the other gifts and vice versa. This brings balance into the world. Don't get caught in looking at the negative side and look for the wonderful attributes that each gift brings.

Which gift am I?

A great place to start is to make a cross on a sheet of paper. On the horizontal line to the left write the word reserved and on the right side write the word direct, on the vertical line at the top write the word open and at the bottom write the word contained.

When answering the questions below, think about when you talk to people you don't know really well, not the people you are really familiar with.

Start with the horizontal line and ask yourself "When I speak to others generally, am I direct or am I more reserved". Do you offer your opinion openly or do you hold back a little? Place a tick on the left side of the page if you are more reserved; place a tick on the right side of the page if you are more direct.

With the vertical line ask yourself "When I am talking to

people do I openly talk about my family and private life or am I more private about those topics?" Do you talk about your family and friends a lot or not? If you openly talk about these topics place a tick at the top of the page, if you are more contained when it comes to these topics place a tick at the bottom of the page.

In the top left square write the word Feeler.

In the bottom left square write Visionary.

In the bottom right square write Leader.

In the top right square write Entertainer.

Look at where you have placed your ticks and identify a box. This will give you an idea of which gift you have as your most developed.

I have already mentioned Florence Littauer and Jerry Clark as two excellent resources to give a deeper understanding and there have been many other books written on the subject. I highly recommend exploring the personalities which will give you further insights into your own gifts, but for now I will stick to the basics so that you may gain a little insight as to how these gifts work and why we are all different.

That old saying "Do unto others as you'd like done to you" may not be necessarily true.

The Feeler (phlegmatic, dove, yellow)

The Feelers fall into the top left square.

A person with this gift works with their feelings. They are generally reserved but open in their sharing with matters including their private life. They are generally lovers of people, animals and the planet. They are very empathetic, quiet and soft in their nature. Because they work with their feelings they can have them hurt easily. These people are more hands on and learn best by doing. They are generally the peace maker in society but don't back them into a corner or they will come out fighting. They are the best nurturers on the planet and make wonderful parents. They are patient, friendly and relaxed. Usually you will find these people working in jobs as nurses, teachers, animal rescue workers or counsellors.

Notes . . .

The Visionary (melancholy, owl, green)

The Visionaries fall into the bottom left square.

A person with this gift works with having a mental picture in their Mind. They are also reserved and do not share their private life openly. They usually don't show their emotions and tend to analyze things first. They are not generally spontaneous people. However, when they make a decision they tend to stick to it. These people tend to learn best by reading or seeing what they need to do or learn. They don't like to be rushed or pushed into a decision before they have had time to think about it or check it out. They are the people who we rely on for all of our research and detail when we need to get things right. They are thoughtful, faithful and persistent. Usually you will find them in jobs such as accountants, architects, engineers and computer programmers.

Notes . . .

The Leader (choleric, eagle, intuitive, red)

The Leaders fall into the bottom right square.

A person with this gift works with the bottom line. They are straight forward and do not share their private life openly. They usually do not get involved in the emotion, just the task at hand and are not side tracked easily. They make the best leaders as they are task and generally money oriented. They say it as it is which may offend or intimidate other personalities although that is not the intention. They like to have the detail of the overall picture but not all of the nitty gritty information in between. These people tend to learn best with their hearing. If you want to get a job done quickly and properly this is the person you need. They are adventurous, persuasive and confident. Usually you will find these people as CEOs of companies and in the corporate world.

Notes . . .

The Entertainer (sanguine, peacock, prophetic, blue)

The Entertainers fall into the top right square.

A person with this gift is very creative, animated and emotional. They are very direct in their speech and very open about everything. They are the life of the party and are very spontaneous. They don't like detail at all and quite often live in organised chaos. They never let the truth get in the way of a good story and often make decisions without thinking it through. They are fun to be around and come up with some wild ideas; however, they can't always see it to completion as another brilliant idea may pop up and change their focus. These people learn best when it is made fun and memorable for them. They are the best promoters in the world. They are cheerful, vivacious and spontaneous. Usually you will find them as actors, artists or working in places that involve fun.

Notes . . .

My Personality

Always be yourself, express yourself and have faith in yourself.

– Bruce Lee

Chapter 7

It's Okay to be Me

The me I see,
is the me I'll be.

It's Okay to be Me

We all have something special about us that we can develop. Some people are good academically and others are good with their hands. Some are good at helping people and others are fantastic at entertaining people. Without the understanding of who you are it could be easy to look at others and compare yourself wondering "Why you can't just be like someone else?" This can be a very dangerous game to play with yourself. It is called "The Grass is Greener Syndrome" it can be very destructive to your self esteem. It can be very easy to beat yourself up mentally when you do this, especially if you ask your Mind disempowering questions.

As I have said previously, the Mind stores data and will look for things to compare. If you were to say "Why am I so stupid?" then your Mind would come up with all of the answers to why you are "so stupid" based on "the stupid things" that you have done in the past. That is exactly what it is, the past. It is important to ask wise questions and allow yourself to work with your Soul to find inspiration in all of the good qualities you have.

A child named Billy may not be as good as his friend Sam academically. What Billy may not realise is that Sam may be advanced in that particular area of learning while Billy may actually be above average. However, if Billy compares himself to Sam he may begin to think of himself as not very smart. Sam on the other hand may also do the same thing and compare himself when Billy's better at working with his hands. Alternatively, if Sam compares himself to Billy he may form the opinion that he is hopeless when it comes to wood work.

We all have different strengths that we were gifted with. We all have something worthwhile to offer. That is how our society works. Some make great doctors and some make great plumbers. If you understand your strengths then you can work with them giving you a more fulfilled feeling inside.

Now is a good time to find out all the great things about you. Why now? Because, it is the next step in unfolding who you are. Take some time to relax and just enjoy being who you are. Sit and listen to your Soul whilst doing this exercise. If you catch yourself questioning something you have come up with then you are listening to your Mind. Disregard the Mind's questioning but write it down anyway.

Make a list of all of the good qualities, strengths and talents that you have. This is not being conceited or bragging. It is good to see that you are a great person and capable of great things. Think of as many as you can. As you continue to read this book, add to your list whenever you think of another quality that you have.

If you are a little stuck ask friends and family what

qualities, strengths and talents they see in you. Again, do not listen to the questioning Mind, just write them down. You may find out some pretty neat things about yourself.

I am so happy and grateful that *I* am . . .

_____

_____

_____

_____

_____

_____

_____

I hope you found out some great qualities, strengths and talents that you didn't realise you had. This may now give you a better perspective on what personality and gifts you have if you had not already worked it out. Depending on the gift that you have you will work differently with your Body, Mind and Soul to someone who has a different gift from you.

I remember when I learnt about the personalities and gifts that I have and thinking to myself "Oh, so that's why I do that". It made me feel more comfortable and I then began to develop my talents which are unique to me. It also gave me a better appreciation of others. I now watch in amazement at some of the skills that other people have. I can appreciate and respect them for who they are without feeling envy and I am able to complement them on their wonderful skills.

One thing to remember when you are learning about the personalities is NEVER label anyone else as they may be upset by this. This information is for you, to help you understand yourself. It is also to help you to understand others so that you may have better relationships. If they ask what gift you think they might be then it is more empowering for them to work it out with your help so that they can understand themselves better.

When you know what gift others are you can treat them as they like to be treated, keep in mind it may not necessarily be the way that you like to be treated. If you are a visionary for example and you are talking to a feeler don't give them nitty gritty details, when you are with an entertainer try to loosen up a little and when you are with a leader make sure to get to the point without the need to fill in all the detail. A leader will be happy to ask for more detail if they need it.

It's Okay to be Me

Chapter 8

My Feelings

My Feelings

Now that you have a better understanding of the Body, Mind & Soul and that your thoughts can have an effect on your feelings, it is time to start looking at how that can affect the way you move through life. Let's start with understanding what feelings are about.

There are lots of words to describe the feelings that we can have. There are feelings of happiness, sadness, anger, fear, jealousy and the list goes on. All of these feelings fit into two categories. They are either positive which make you feel good or negative which does not make you feel good.

Feelings can be indicators as to whether or not we are on track. Negative feelings generally come from negative thoughts. A person who is negative in their thoughts tends to only see negative things, which makes them feel bad. They can become addicted to these feelings and thoughts and will then tend to see more negativity. These people are usually caught in their Mind. A positive feeling followed up by a negative thought can also quickly turn into a negative feeling.

If you allow yourself to get stuck listening to your Mind you can rob yourself of opportunities that your Soul is trying to share with you. Let's take the example of a holiday.

My Feelings

If you plan a holiday and listen to your Soul you may think of all the different places that you can go and of all the different things that you can do. The whole experience will be one big adventure. Because you are open to hearing suggestions then you may be guided towards something you didn't expect. You never know what may happen, I personally know quite a few people who have met the love of their life overseas, married them and are living very happy lives.

Alternatively, if you get caught in the Mind you may think of terrorists taking over your plane. The feelings of excitement can turn into anxiety very quickly. That in turn will lead to another negative thought and before you know it there are a million and one negative experiences filling your head for no good reason at all. It might end up seeming daunting and you may begin to question going on the trip after all. The chances of any of these experiences ever happening are slim but the fear can take over and rob you of the whole exciting experience of the trip. Powerful how the Mind works, isn't it.

I'm not saying that the mind is a bad thing as it does a wonderful job of collecting, storing and retrieving information. Just be clear that you are recalling the right information. This comes with practice. Learn to ask positive questions.
Since thoughts can alter feelings it would be wise to catch yourself out having negative thoughts when

you don't feel so good. When you get involved in the emotion it is easy to get away from the true facts. The following technique can help you to sort the feelings from the facts.

Pat Mesiti says "If someone spits on you they don't make you angry, they make you wet!" I am the one who allows myself to feel anger or disgust or . . or . . or . . . the list goes on. I was a little disturbed by that when I first heard it. After some thought I came to realise that others' behavior is their stuff but how I react to their behavior is my stuff.

Sorting the Feelings from the Facts.

These questions can be used to look at any experience, be it positive or negative. This will help you to see if it is a distorted view that you have of the experience. If you have a good experience or result it is good to look at what worked so that you can repeat it. If you recognise that you are having negative experiences you can use these questions to help you to analyse what is going on for you.

1. What did *I* do / what happened?
2. What did *I* learn?
3. What could *I* do differently next time?
4. What was *my* highlight?

Remember there is always going to be positive and negative experiences in your life. How would you know that you were having a good day if you hadn't had a bad day? It is all in how you look at it and what you choose to call the experience. A negative experience isn't necessarily bad. It can be an opportunity for a great learning experience. Let's look at an example using the questions to sort out the facts and look for the learning in the experience.

1. **What did I do?**
I yelled at my children for getting covered in mud and making my floors dirty.

2. **What did I learn?**
That my children love exploring and being outdoors. They really enjoy themselves playing in the mud which gives me time for myself. Mud is not really harmful.

3. **What could I do differently next time?**
Make sure that they are wearing old clothes and they strip off their clothes in the laundry and clean themselves up a bit before coming in the house.

4. **What was my highlight?**
Seeing the proud looks on their faces all covered in mud as they asked me to come and see their mud pies.

After looking at the answers to the questions it then gives an opportunity to go and apologise to the children for yelling at them and set boundaries so that everyone has a better experience next time. They are children after all.

Changing my feelings

Although our thoughts can create our feelings there are many ways to alter our feelings. Hunch your shoulders over and bow your head down. Think of something sad. It doesn't feel very good does it? You probably can't breathe as well either.

Now put your head up, lift your shoulders back, take a deep breath and laugh. Feels very different, doesn't it.

We can make choices to alter our mood if we can learn to catch ourselves when we are having negative thoughts or feelings. You can follow it up by asking yourself the question. **"So what would *I* like?"** This will allow you then to focus on the positive and get yourself back on track.

It might be that you would like to see the positive in the experience. That is where you can use the questions in the last technique. This will give you the information to be able to do what I call "re-frame" the experience.

To re-frame is like changing the frame on a picture.

My Feelings

Have you ever tried to find a frame for a special photo? You may find a timber frame which looks okay but it doesn't feel quite right. If you put a metal frame on it the picture may look entirely different and make you feel really good when you look at the picture. The same is with your life. You may look at a situation or circumstance in a certain way which might not make you feel so good. When you decide to put a different frame on it and look at the picture from a different point of view you may feel differently about what happened.

I used a re-frame in the example with the questions in the last technique. I said "They really enjoy themselves playing in the mud which gives me time for myself. Mud is not really harmful". It is amazing how re-framing can change the way you feel.

Music can also alter our mood in either a positive or negative way. Like tuning in to different frequencies of radio stations we can Tune Into different vibrations of moods. One piece of music or lyrics can make you feel sad, anxious or angry. A different piece can make you feel joy, excitement or motivation. It's your choice. What do you want to Tune Into?

The next time you find yourself wanting to "navel-gaze" because you feel "bad", make the choice to change your vibration to a positive one and get back in touch with the Soul part of you. Read from an uplifting book, dance to your favorite music, look at pictures of what you desire, think about what makes you happy, excited and motivated or read your **Regrouping Diary.** We will explore the diary later in the book.

What are some things that *I* can do when *I* am in a negative vibration to change it into a positive vibration?

_____

_____

_____

_____

_____

Once you are feeling positive and you can think clearly, sit down and sort the facts from the feelings. It will be easier to make decisions when you are not stuck in the emotion. You may also want to re-frame the situation.

If you are on anti-depressants then it is a great time while you are feeling good to work on yourself and your feelings. You may find that you may be able to wean yourself off the drugs eventually. This would need to happen with your practitioner's support of course.

Chapter 9

My Choices

My Choices

I spoke about making choices in regards to changing how you feel in the previous chapter "My Feelings".

There are always choices to be made in life. Most often making a choice will create a change. I see change as a good thing. I believe it is usually for the better.

If you are working with the facts it makes it easier to make decisions based on understanding rather than with emotion alone.

When I was working for a boss, I knew that if I became unhappy at work I had choices. I could choose to sort out the problem, change my attitude towards it or leave. Sometimes I made what I called "dumb" choices and sometimes I felt great for the choice I made. The key is there are no "dumb" choices, just opportunities to learn from. As I have already said, I believe change is usually for the better even though it may not look that way at the time. Realise it for what it is and learn from what happened, use the knowledge you gain to take you closer to your goals and dreams. It may be as simple as saying "I'm not gonna do that again". It may also require a choice to think differently about how the situation is viewed by re-framing.

I see life as a series of games and choices. Take the game

of Monopoly for example. You choose to play the game, you might not like all of the rules, like going to jail, but if you want to play the game those are the rules you follow. So you make a choice to play the game and you have a great time. If you are no longer enjoying the game, what do you do? You pack up the game and find something else to do. You may even decide to make up your own game with your own rules. You always have choices. The same can apply to your life.

When faced with a choice in life it is good to ask questions which will help to make a decision. Start by drawing a line down the center of a sheet of paper. Place "Fors" on one side and "Againsts" on the other side. Think of as many positives and reasons as to why you should make the decision and place them under the "Fors" and all of the reasons why not or negatives under the "Againsts" heading. This will give you a clearer picture of what you are working with. You can then work with the facts rather than with the emotion. Here are some great questions to ask which may help with this process . . .

1. What would *I* like?
What would I like the outcome to be?

2. Is this going to take me in the direction in which *I* want to go?
If the answer to the second question is "yes" great. If the answer is no then the question is.

My Choices

Am *I* still going to do this or not?
I know when you have a family to feed and rent or a mortgage to pay, you may feel like you don't have choices at times. You <u>always</u> have choices. That choice may be to stay where you are for the moment while you actively look for something else. It's good to remember that you have choices. Use the knowledge that you have of your Mind and your Soul to help you with your decision making process.

There are not many weeks in the year – only 52. When I reach 60 years of age that would only equate to 3120 weeks. Wow, a week can go by so quickly and how many have I wasted to date? I **choose** not to waste my weeks. I **choose** to live my life to the full rather than waiting for things to work out some day. What are you waiting for? The thing is you never know how many weeks you have left.

Think back to the Thredbo accident in 1997 where a ski lodge collapsed under a land slide killing 18 people. After 65 hours one man was pulled out alive. Stuart Diver survived the collapse; his wife had perished next to him. The night before when he and his wife Sally went to bed they would never had dreamed that their time might be up. They were young, married and living their dreams on the ski slopes of Thredbo. In an instant that was taken away for Sally anyway. Stuart then had a choice to make. He chose to survive and did what was necessary to have that happen until help arrived.

My Choices

Sometimes the key is realising there is a choice to be made.

Some people experience mental torture when they are faced with a decision. I hear people saying things like "I'm a battler" and I ask myself "Why are they choosing that? Why are they choosing to let life be a battle?" Sometimes in life we can be faced with a situation that may cause an internal struggle.

A man wants to spend more time with his children but is getting a business started. He knows all the reasons as to why he should spend more time with his children but the business is at the stage where it requires a lot of his time. In this situation unless he makes a decision he can be torn between his work and his family and it may end up causing friction in both areas of his life. He can however make a choice to have both. Once he makes this decision he will then be able to think of ways that he can have both. That is where the Soul can help with providing inspiration when a decision has been made.

One way could be that he has a conversation with his wife and family explaining that he has to put a priority onto the business for the next so many months. He could then schedule into his diary, appointments for a couple of hours a few times a week or a day each week for family time, where he completely forgets about work while he is on "family time". By doing this he doesn't spend his time at work thinking about the family and his time with the family thinking about work. He can then be more productive at work and enjoy being with the family. Life doesn't have to be a struggle.

By living life the way you choose rather than the way you think you have to can free yourself of a mental struggle. A weight can be lifted by honoring your needs and making choices that do not compromise your values. By allowing others to honor their values and needs takes just as much courage. Being without judgment and allowing others to do what is right for them and allowing yourself to do what it right for you makes far more harmonious relationships.

Bob Proctor in his book **"You Were Born Rich"** tells the John and Pat Swanson story. Pat and John wanted a house and told Bob that they couldn't afford a home and they didn't have a deposit. Bob told them that they didn't need a deposit. When they questioned him as to why, Bob told Pat and John that they didn't need one because they hadn't decided to buy a house yet. They made the decision to buy a home, so they went looking and found the one that they loved and put in an offer. This put the pressure on as they had to find the deposit. With faith they listened to inspiration, everything fell into place and they came up with the money on time. They made a choice to have a house and they then took the necessary steps to turn it into a reality.

My Choices

I choose to enjoy life.

I choose to live free from depressing thoughts and feelings.

I choose to go for and live my dreams.

What are you choosing? What are you fearful of not choosing? What do you do because you feel you have to? Complete the exercise and make some choices for You.

What do *I* do because *I* feel *I* have to?

_____

_____

_____

Who am *I* doing it for?

_____

_____

_____

What would happen if *I* chose not to?

_____

_____

_____

My Choices

So what do *I* want?

_____

_____

_____

What am *I* choosing now?

_____

_____

_____

How does it make *me* feel?

_____

_____

_____

Is there anything *I* need to re-frame?

_____

_____

_____

Knowing that you have the choice is a wonderful feeling. I know what I choose. Write down a few choices that you have decided to make.

My Choices

***I* choose** _____

A success is one who
decided to succeed
– and worked.

A failure is one who
decided to succeed
– and wished.

A decided failure is one
who failed to decide
– and waited.

– William A Ward

Chapter 10

My Beliefs

My Beliefs

The dictionary states: **belief** – acceptance of any received theology: acceptance (of thing, fact, statement, etc.) as true or existing.

I have spoken in previous chapters about beliefs. Just like habits, beliefs are stored in your Mind. They are similar and can be formed in many ways, from things that you were told to experiences that you have had. I have heard it said by many people that in the middle of every be**lie**f there is a **lie**. Let's look at that a little closer so that you can understand your Mind a little better.

A belief is only true if it is true for you. A belief may serve you for a period of time and then you may choose to change the belief. You may be thinking "Why would I want to change something that I know to be true?" There may be a difference between a belief and the truth. Let's look at some examples

Pre 194 BC many cultures believed that the world was flat. It was then discovered that the world was not flat, it was round. Some people had a difficult time comprehending that the world was round and chose to keep their belief that the world was flat. They thought that the discovery was nonsense. Others chose to change their belief with the new knowledge that the world is round. The Truth as we now know it is that the earth is round. With the new knowledge and the facts global belief changed.

Each individual has their own beliefs about certain events, objects and experiences. It is our right to have free thinking. It does not necessarily mean that we are right. There is the truth and there is a belief which is not necessarily founded on the truth.

Let's say a little girl was bitten by a dog. It could be easy for her to form the belief that all dogs bite people. The data or information from the attack is stored in the Mind as a memory and forms a belief. Each time the little girl comes near a dog after that day what do you think might be happening in her Mind? The mind will look for any past data to do with dogs, remember the attack and send a chemical reaction through her Body which will be felt in the form of fear. Is the fear real? Absolutely! The Mind works to "protect us" but is the little girl living a distorted truth because of her belief that all dogs bite?

Unless the little girl chooses to change the belief or gets the knowledge that helps her to see the truth, that not every dog is going to bite her, then the belief in her Mind can cause her pain for the rest of her life.

Let me take you on a little journey that paints a picture of how you can look at all of your habits, beliefs and memories kept in your Mind.

Imagine the Mind as a sack with the top gathered with strong elastic. You want to open the bag and explore what beliefs, habits and memories are in there.

It takes practice to learn to open the bag and look at the contents to see what is running your life. At first you pull at the elastic to try and look at what is in the bag but it is dark. You stick your hand in the bag to pull out a belief, habit or memory and it may be scary because you are not sure what you are going to find.

It's important to know that it is all okay. Take the courage to look in the bag as you may be surprised at what you pull out. It may be a beautiful butterfly. This could be where people often told you how clever you were. You would make sure you put the butterfly back in the bag as you want to keep that belief. It may be an interesting caterpillar. This is where you might have been told that boys have to play with cars and girls have to play with dolls. You can look at it and say isn't that interesting, do I really want to keep that belief? You may choose to put the caterpillar back in the bag or you can let it go and tell it that you no longer need it.

There may be some poisonous snakes in your bag. They will lie in the bottom without a problem until the bag is shaken and they will rear up spitting poison. You may have been told "Don't be so dumb". That poison may

My Beliefs

make you feel really bad and even affect your physical Body in some way. Once you catch the snake you definitely want to release it and let it go.

You may carry your sack on your back and the sack may become heavy. When you think negatively about the caterpillars you could feed them, which makes them bigger, they may even turn into snakes. However, you may find when you pull them out of the sack; they are smaller than you thought. The fear of dogs from the little girl I described earlier would be what I would call a snake for the little girl. That is definitely something that she would want to take out of her bag of beliefs if she doesn't want to be always looking over her shoulder.

We are very fortunate these days to live in the information age. Information is at our fingertips. All we need to do is get onto a computer or look in a book and search for the answers that we require. When we are searching it is important to ensure that the information is coming from a reputable source.

For many years during the 20th century people believed that cigarettes were good for you. They were encouraged to smoke them during the war years to calm their nerves. Movies were made during that time and it was very fashionable or you could say "cool" to smoke.

Once people began to experience ill health and addictions, smoking was questioned. The tobacco

My Beliefs

companies continued to say that smoking was not bad for your health and tried, quite successfully, for some time to squash what they called "rumors". All the information that we know now proves that smoking is bad for your health. So, why are so many people still smoking? Maybe the young people are still forming the belief that it is "cool" to smoke. Or maybe they are just choosing to smoke.

What beliefs do you have? Are they truth? Do they serve you?

In this exercise write down 10 beliefs that you know you have, that you believe to be true. Go to the internet or library and research or ask an authority on the subject until you have enough information to know if it is the truth. (When I said Authority I meant that you wouldn't ask a plumber how to fix your appendicitis although the plumber would have an opinion on the subject it may not be the correct information.)

Once you have found the truth ask yourself **"does it still serve *me* to believe this?"** Only then do you have all of the information to make a decision whether to keep the belief or choose to reject it.

My Beliefs

Beliefs

1. _____
   _____

   True / False _____ Accept / Reject _____

2. _____
   _____

   True / False _____ Accept / Reject _____

3. _____
   _____

   True / False _____ Accept / Reject _____

4. _____
   _____

   True / False _____ Accept / Reject _____

5. _____
   _____

   True / False _____ Accept / Reject _____

My Beliefs

6. _____
   _____

True / False _____ Accept / Reject _____

7. _____
   _____

True / False _____ Accept / Reject _____

8. _____
   _____

True / False _____ Accept / Reject _____

9. _____
   _____

True / False _____ Accept / Reject _____

10. _____
    _____

True / False _____ Accept / Reject _____

My Beliefs

I am not saying that you should go and overhaul your Mind. As I have said before life is a continual process. If you continue to expand your knowledge of yourself then you will discover yourself. Take notice of the feelings. If they do not feel so good then maybe there is something that you can look at.

I have given you a number of techniques to work out the facts and be able to find the truth so that you can change the beliefs and habits that are stored in your Mind. You may even want to reframe some of the beliefs around your memories. Sometimes like the story of the pothole in the road it might take a few times to reprogram your Mind with the new habit or belief.

The next poem is what I believe to be a perfect example of how the Mind works. See the change as a good thing and use the techniques to move towards a happier and healthier life.

I am your constant companion,
I am your greatest helper or heaviest burden,
I will push you onward or drag you down
to failure, I am completely at your command.

Half the things you do you might
as well turn over to me,
and I will be able to do them quickly
and correctly.

My Beliefs

I am easily managed,
You must merely be firm with me.

Show me exactly how you want something done,
and after a few lessons I will do it automatically.

I am the servant of all great Men,
and alas of all failures.

As wealth, those who are great I have made great,
those who are failures I have made failures.

I am not a machine,
although I work with the precision of a machine,
plus the intelligence of a Man.

You may run me for profit or run me for ruin,
it makes no difference to me.

Take me, train me, be firm with me,
and I will place the world at your feet.

Be easy with me, and I will destroy you.

Who am I?

I am Habit.

Chapter 11

My Past

"What are the thieves that rob us of today, yesterday and tomorrow? What will all the worrying about yesterday do to change today? Tomorrow is a promissory note at best; all we have is the present, that's why it is called a gift."

– Bob Moawad

My Past

Who we are today is a reflection of our thoughts, feelings and actions in the past. However, who we will be tomorrow is an entirely different matter. As I have discussed in previous chapters, you have the ability to choose. I also gave you techniques to work with how you feel.

There is no difference with your past.

You may have fond memories of your past. These are the sort of memories that you may treasure. There may be things that you are not proud of in your past or you may not be entirely happy with where you are today. As we discovered earlier they may just be a distorted view anyway. If you look for the facts or the real truth, what you perceived to have happened may be different to what actually happened.

Just as your Mind works to form habits, it can form beliefs on something that you tell yourself over and over and over. The saying goes "tell yourself a lie often enough and you will begin to believe it".

Someone may have had their father leave when they were a child. It is quite possible that they formed a belief around what happened based on parts of conversations that they overheard or things that were said to them. If they went on a fact finding mission they may find that the reason their father left and never contacted them again was for an entirely different reason. At times, loved ones say certain things to children to (in their Mind) "protect them from the truth".

Finding the truth will always give you the facts to work with. Sometimes it takes being a little uncomfortable to create change. All that you need to do is make a decision to change. Let go of the things in the past that have been holding you back.

We all have things happen in our life. Holding on to the negative memories from your past does not serve anyone or any purpose. If, as a child, someone told you that you were not going to amount to anything would you like that to be your reality in the future?

You may feel anger or resentment towards someone who has done you wrong or guilt over what you feel you may have done wrong. Ultimately who do these thoughts and feelings effect? I'm sure it is not the other person as they have probably forgotten about it or are too busy thinking about their own stuff. My Grandmother was a wise woman when she said "The only thing you get from looking back is a sore neck".

Some people have had horrific things happen to them in their life so I am not suggesting that you pretend that it didn't happen. However, if it is no longer happening to you now, why would you want to continue to have it in your life? Seek a professional counsellor who can help you to work through what you need to, in order to let it go. I am not suggesting you go to find someone or something to blame and you don't have to condone the actions of the person who did you wrong, but you can choose to let it go.

I know I have said it often throughout the book but change is usually for the better. Someone's Mind may now be saying "How could my partner walking out on me be for the better?" Well maybe the relationship was not so great. Deep down inside maybe you were hoping it would get better. Maybe your partner leaving was what will make it better. What can you learn from the experience that will make you stronger and wiser? How can being stronger and wiser be worse? Re-frame it if you have to.

Letting go is getting rid of the emotion attached to it so that if the subject is brought up, there are no longer the negative thoughts and feelings to go with it. Stop worrying about things that you can no longer change, what is done is done. The person you were then is not the person you are now. You do not deserve to live in the past because your future can be whatever you decide to create.

You may be thinking "well, that's okay to say, but this

My Past

person did this and that person did that, why should I forgive them?" You can't fix anyone else. However, you can fix you. You are not responsible for other people's actions.

A lady who I will call Jane was often upset by her sister. Jane would tell me that her sister had said something that upset her or had done something that Jane thought was not right. Jane also felt that her sister didn't listen to her. I asked Jane "Do you listen to your sister?" There was silence.

Jane had a belief that her sister had not done or said the right thing, Jane realised she was judging her sister's actions on what she thought was the right way for her sister to treat her. Her sister wasn't treating her badly intentionally. Her sister didn't know how Jane wanted to be treated and was probably feeling frustrated herself. By expecting something that her sister didn't know how to give, Jane was setting herself up for disappointment.

Jane made a decision to forgive her sister and in the process forgave herself for the way that she was feeling about her sister. By forgiving, Jane then opened herself up to having a clearer communication with her sister. Jane later reported back that her sister had "changed" and they were getting along fantastically. I would say that Jane "changed" how she felt about her sister which allowed her sister to have a better relationship with her.

It may be that you are no longer in communication with the person who hurt you. Maybe you could write them a letter then burn the letter. Let the Universe take care of the rest.

Make a decision to let go of the negative feelings that you have about your past. Forgive all of the resentment or guilt that you hold. Forgive yourself for holding onto these feelings that no longer serve you.

Release any person from your past that you have negative thoughts and feelings about. Release them to their higher good. Wish them health, happiness and prosperity. Release yourself to your higher good for a healthier, happier and prosperous life. Let the past stay in the past.

Forgiveness affirmation

*I*_____

willingly forgive all of the resentment and guilt in *my* life which has filled *my* head and heavied *my* heart.

I release_____

to their higher good. I wish them health, happiness and prosperity. I release *me* to mine, for a healthier, happier and prosperous life.

Signed_____ Date _____

Chapter 12

Where am I now?

Where am I now?

Now is probably a great time to take a look at what you have learnt about yourself and the few techniques on how the Mind works. Before I move onto working with the Soul part of you it is time to take an honest look at yourself. It's okay. Relax, it is another simple exercise that will give you more understanding so that you can make the changes you are looking for.

Let's recap on the basics. You and I are Souls having a physical experience. We are gifted with a Body and intellect (Mind). These are the parts that make up the whole. One does not function without the other two. How would you think to kick the ball with your Body without your Mind? What would give you the inspiration to play ball without your Soul. We are where we are now having a physical experience and we call it Life.

Life is always changing, nothing stays the same. We are either moving forward or we are moving backwards. We are in a positive vibration or a negative vibration. You could say you are feeling good or feeling bad, you are getting results or not getting results. It doesn't really matter where you are at now in any area of your life because you can change direction in a second with a single thought or action. What is important to know is where you are really at and how you feel about where you are at.

Where am I now?

If I was going to drive from Melbourne to Sydney I would have to first know where I was so that I could look up the maps and work out how to get there.

Truly knowing where you are at takes being honest with yourself. It's like an alcoholic who needs to recognise that they have a problem and state "I AM AN ALCOHOLIC" before they can begin to work on a solution. It takes being honest with yourself.

To be vulnerable is to open yourself up and be honest with your feelings. That is your doubts, fears and any concerns that you have in a particular area of your life. It is only yourself that you have to be honest with. The purpose of this exercise is not for you to give yourself a hard time. It is to be used as a datum point. Once you can identify the areas that you would like to work on and the results you are getting in that particular area of your life then you are able to make decisions. You can then connect with the Soul part of you to give you inspiration to get the results you desire.

I believe that you are in the perfect place at the moment. You are reading this book and you will move yourself in a positive direction. It is time to look at where you are at and how you feel about it. This way you can see if it is a distorted view or not and give you the ability to work with the facts or find the truth so that you have a clearer understanding.

Take some time to understand where you are at in the different areas of your life.

How do you feel? Do you have any doubts or concerns or do you feel fulfilled. List as much information as you can. Play some music if you need to or sit in a quiet space so that you can connect with your Soul and allow the inspiration to flow.

Where am I with my . . .

Career? _____

_____

_____

Relationships? _____

_____

_____

Financial State? _____

_____

_____

Where am I now?

Health? _____
_____
_____

Fitness? _____
_____
_____

Mental State? _____
_____
_____

Marriage? _____
_____
_____

Other? _____
_____
_____

Where am I now?

Before anything else, getting ready is the secret to success.

– Henry Ford

Chapter 13

What am I expecting?

What am I expecting?

You may desire to have, do or be something in life and may have even been using an affirmation to achieve it, but in your Mind you expect something else. For example, you may desire to get a deposit together for a house quickly; however, you may really expect that it will take some time to get the money together. Some people call this being realistic. To me realistic is what is real to you. This is usually when you look at your current circumstances rather than putting a plan in place, then going out and creating what you really want.

If you think it will take a long time to save a deposit for a house then it will. The reason for this is because you have formed a belief that it will take you a long time. What will end up happening is sub-consciously you will find ways to use the money that you want to save on other things and the excuses that you have for spending that money will seem reasonable.

On the other hand, if you were to focus on having the money quickly, writing an affirmation that sets a date for when you want to have the deposit, then once you learn how to work with the Soul part of you, you will come up with all sorts of ideas as to how to save or obtain the money. You may even happen to mention what your goal is to someone who may in some way help you or give you a suggestion of how to raise the amount of money that you need.

What am I expecting?

If you do not have the **feeling** of belief, along with the words that you are saying, how can you hope to achieve it? The Soul part of you works with the feeling; if the feeling is contradicting the thought then they cancel each other out. You must truly believe that it will be yours. Let's say you want to find a new partner who has certain attributes. You must believe and feel that you deserve to have it or your Mind may do things to push it away by not seeing that person even if they are standing right there in front of you. I will explain more about this in the chapter "What am I attracting?"

Let's look at the truth. There are millions of people meeting their ideal partner every day.

Why not you?

If you believe this then you will be open to seeing that person when he/she comes along. If you don't believe they will come along then you are absolutely right. Your perfect partner will be there however; you will not see him/her or you may do something to sabotage the relationship. Does the unexpected happen? Sure, as I said change is usually good. I know that you will find a solution if you choose to go for your dreams. The answers are inside you.

Take the time to look at your desires and what you have been expecting in different areas of your life. Are they the same? Then I will show you how to work with the Soul part of you to get what you are expecting.

What am I expecting?

What have I been expecting with....

Career? _____

_____

Relationships? _____

_____

Financial State? _____

_____

Health? _____

_____

Fitness? _____

_____

Mental State? _____

_____

Marriage? _____

_____

What am I expecting?

My Spirituality? _____

_____

_____

My Children? _____

_____

_____

Other? _____

_____

_____

Expect the results that you want in your life. When you expect then you can powerfully choose what you think and feel. This will create the actions necessary for better results in your life.

What am I expecting?

We tend to live up to our expectations.

– Earl Nightingale

Chapter 14

What am I attracting?

What am I attracting?

We have talked briefly about your Body which science has taught us so much about. I have shared a lot about and introduced you to some techniques to work with your Mind. In this chapter I am going to help you have more insight into working with your Soul.

Life is happening all around you right now. There are millions of things going on, noises and what you could term stimuli everywhere. For a moment or two take the time to stop and listen to the birds outside. As I am writing it is early in the morning and I am aware that there are hundreds of birds chirping away, possibly thousands. It is quite a nice feeling when I stop and just listen. If you are sitting reading this at night, the birds have probably gone to bed. Focus on the ticking of the clock or listen for other noises that you notice. You have just "Tuned In" to some of the things in life that are going on around you at the moment. Are you finding it a little distracting now while you are trying to read? See if you can now block the noise by "tuning out" and tune back in to your reading. If you are having trouble tuning back in, take a break for a few minutes. Go and grab something to drink and settle back because I am about to share some important clues which will help you to work with your Soul.

How cool is that! There is a wonderful part to your

What am I attracting?

brain that helps you to Tune In and out. This part of the brain is called the Amygdala and filtering is part of its function.

The Amygdala is the part of the brain that receives stimuli from most of the Body's sensory systems (touch, smell, taste, sound etc). It is responsible for processing and memorising emotional reactions. It works like a filter blocking out things you do not require, Hmm, or not want to hear. It can also do the opposite by lifting the filter to what you want to see or hear. If you saw, heard, smelt and sensed everything that was going on around you then you might go into overload. Personally I think that I would go insane. This is another great way that your Mind "protects" you. What you learnt in previous chapters, which was explained beautifully by the poem on habit, is that your Mind can be your maker or destroyer.

Let's use another example here so that you are clear with how the "filter" works. For this exercise I do not want you to cheat or you will not have the full effect of the exercise. Without looking up from your book listen to my instructions. The first thing that I am going to get you to do is look around the room that you are in. Not yet! If you have already looked then you don't get to look again. I don't want you to read past this paragraph before you look around the room and when you think you know the room that you are sitting in you may read the next paragraph.

What am I attracting?

There is no cheating here either. Without looking around the room, I want you to think of all the things that you can think of that are red in the room. Once you have done that you can look around the room and see how many things that you can notice that are red. Of course this can work with any color but I chose red for the purpose of the exercise.

Pretty cool isn't it to see the red. It is like it is jumping out at you. That is because you "Tuned In" to what you wanted to see. The red things were always there but you probably didn't notice. You didn't notice because you didn't need to.

Now we get to the exciting part of bridging the Mind and the Soul. This is where the Law of Attraction comes in. To attract what you want into your life you must use the skill of "tuning in".

What you Tune Into is what you will notice. Have you ever seen a car you really liked or been looking for a house and all of a sudden you see that car everywhere or for sale signs all over the place?

I have heard women when they think they might be pregnant or want to start trying for a baby, comment on how they see pregnant women and babies everywhere. The babies, cars and for sale signs were probably always there but you had never noticed them because that is not what you were looking for so your Mind filtered them out.

What am I attracting?

This is where you need to be clear that your Soul will give you the inspiration to notice what is in front of you. If you are not listening because you are caught in your Mind then you are going to miss the opportunity that is being presented to you.

It reminds me of a tale which explains why we don't always see the opportunities knocking at our door. This can happen when we imagine the opportunity in a different form from the way it may be presented to us.

There was a city which had a major flood. A man was blocked in his house as water poured in up to his waist. A couple came past in a dingy and called through the window "Hop in and we will get you to safe ground" the man replied "No thank you, God will save me". After a while the man was forced into the upper level of his house with the water rising fast. A state emergency launch went past and called to the man to hop in the launch. The man replied "No thank you, God will save me". Before he knew it he was sitting on the roof of his house when a police helicopter flew overhead, dropped a rope and a voice on the mega phone said "grab the rope and we will tow you to safety" to which the man replied "No thank you, God will save me". Of course the man perished and when he saw God he was very angry. "Why didn't you save me?" the man yelled to which God replied "I sent you a boat, a launch and a helicopter. What more did you want?" He wasn't open to see the help as he believed that it would appear in the form of "God".

What am I attracting?

The Soul is always for expansion so it may point you in the direction of something even better than you imagined so it is important to be open to see it when it is there. This is why it is not important to listen to the Mind when it starts to question. If you are not sure, Tune In to your Soul if you need to. Ask your Soul questions and it will answer quickly. Take the first thing that comes to your head as usually the Mind steps in next and begins to question or give you possible alternatives. If you listen you will begin to notice the difference between the two voices. The Soul will provide positive ideas or inspiration and the Mind will usually question or provide negative feedback. If you are thinking "What voice" that is the voice of your questioning Mind. Learn to "Tune In" to what the Soul is saying. Listen for positive ideas and inspiration.

I am not suggesting that you speak out loud when you are communicating with your Mind or Soul. It is an internal dialogue. If we all walked around chatting to ourselves out loud it would get very confusing. If you are thinking "I'm not going to talk to myself" well you just did. You might as well make it positive talk.

Back to the Law of "Attraction".

Because your Soul is connected to everything then that is how your Soul may "Tune In" to another Soul or thing in order to set up what you need. I watched this happen to a friend of mine not so long ago. This lady had identified that she was not very patient. Be careful what you ask for. If you ask for patience you will be given opportunities to learn patience.

We were out getting a cup of coffee when my friend tutted and said "Does that happen to you?" She began to tell me that a lady had walked in front of her and then stopped. My friend then continued to explain that people pull in front of her when she is driving, then they slow down, which frustrated her.

I remember giggling and asked "Do you think their Soul communicated with your Soul to give you opportunities to learn patience?" My friend giggled back and replied "Well I'm not getting it am I!" The lady who walked in front of my friend probably had the inspiration to change direction, moved and probably wondered why the person behind her was tutting.

This can be very powerful when you learn to "Tune In" to what you need to do, be or have to get what you are looking for in life. You can "Tune In" to anything whether you are conscious to it or not.

Knowing that, it makes sense to say that when you have negative thoughts or feelings then you would be "Tuning In" to the negative. As a consequence you will only tend to see all of the negative or "bad" things that are happening around or to you. This could make you feel worse and you could Tune In to more negative stuff and it would continue as a cycle until you chose to break the cycle.

What am I attracting?

When you feel good and think happy thoughts you would "Tune In" to all of the positive things around you. That's when everything seems to go your way and it makes you feel fantastic. The cycle would repeat itself in a positive way. These are the times when you should be mindful of what your desires are, in order to attract them as that is exactly what you will "Tune In" to.

One thing I would like to point out again is life can't be "great" all of the time. How would you know a good day if you didn't have an average day once in a while? There are positives and negatives in life. It is all a matter of perception. It is about living with more balance so that the ups are not too up and the downs are not too down. Less emotion in your life will allow you to see truth more clearly. This is why I have given you the techniques throughout the book so that you have the tools at hand to train your Mind. When you have your Mind under control you can spend more time "Tuning In" to what your Soul is trying to tell you.

It is therefore important to never hate something more than you love its opposite. If you focus on what you don't want you will get more of what you are focusing on. Place the focus onto what you do want and you will find around you what you need to hear, do or have to move in the direction of your desire.

Ask wise questions from your Mind and Soul. If you ask silly questions like "Why am I so stupid?" then you are going to get all of the answers to why. Think of asking questions that encourage wise answers. You could use questions like . . .

How can I . . . ?
What do I need to do, know, be or have to . . . ?

Think of some more ways that you can ask questions that will encourage your Soul to inspire you. Then you need to be open to hearing the inspiration.

Do not try to force the answers because that will shut down the filter process. If you relax and "Tune In" then you will be open to hear what your Soul is trying to tell you.

It would be like someone driving around a car park frantically looking for a space and getting frustrated. I have stood in car parks and watched people as they have driven past cars which were just leaving their car space. They are so worked up that they have shut off their filter and ability to work with their Soul. If they stopped relaxed and looked for the truth which is the fact that people come and go from car parks all of the time they would open the channel back up and be able to hear the inspiration and see what is in front of them. Their Soul may say "Don't turn down this lane, go to the next one" and if they drive calmly they will see that someone is about to leave and will get their car park. I always thank my Soul in a fun way for the car park that I find. As I

What am I attracting?

drive in I see a parking space and say "Thanks Grace for the wonderful car space!" It then confirms the habit / belief that I have built into my Mind that I always find a great car space and always feel good.

Beliefs and habits can inhibit the attraction process. By "Tuning in" your Mind and Soul can help you to see the habit or belief. In the "Suggested use" chapter I spoke about the "Blind Spot" which is the habit or belief that you don't know you have. When you are open to seeing the belief then you will observe (notice) the habit. When you understand what the belief or habit is then you are able to change it.

Let's use the example of someone who believes that they are unlovable and does not realise that they have that belief (the blind spot). If someone said to them "You look beautiful today" in their Mind they may say something like "you are just saying that to be nice". This would result in a bad feeling. It is known as self sabotage.

If that person made the decision to attract a loving relationship they could "Tune In" to finding answers. Their Soul would give them the inspiration to see the belief that is holding them back and sabotaging their relationships. When the thought "you are just saying that to be nice" comes into their Mind then the Soul might say something like "Did you just hear that?" That person would then be able to see how they "sabotage" themselves and their relationships. *(observation)*

When they can see the belief they can then choose what they want to believe. By continually catching the negative thoughts they can replace them with new thoughts associated with positive feelings which will create a new belief. This will then change the way that they react when given a compliment and change the state of their relationships.

The next step for that person would be to write a list of all of the things that they want in a partner to attract what they want. If they then "Tuned In" their Soul may inspire them to go somewhere and BINGO there they are, the person of their dreams! Oh WOW. I am getting excited even writing this stuff. It is so powerful and when you get it and start working with it your life changes so quickly it is mind blowing.

I want to give you one more example to ensure that you really understand how to "Tune In to attract what you want" before we move on.

Let's say that you were looking at setting up a website and you want to find a good web designer. If you are in good communication with your Soul (because you practice nurturing and working with that part of you) then you may think "I must find out who knows a good designer".

That same afternoon you may be sitting in a café with friends and overhear two people discussing this great web designer. The conversation would have been on the other table anyway, but, normally you would "Tune Out" all the conversations at the other tables. Instead, by "Tuning In" you are open to hearing what you need whether you are conscious of it or not. Your Soul might say "Go and ask them for the number". At this stage you may have to be careful of the naughty puppy in your Mind which might say "Oh, don't go over there. They might think you are rude" or "What will they think?" Yada, yada, yada.

Take some courage and listen to your Soul. Go over and say "Excuse me, did I just overhear you mention a website designer because I am looking for a good one at the moment". What do you think that person is going to say? They will probably spend the next 5 minutes raving and telling you all about the designer. If not what is the worst that they can do. Say "No, go away" and look you up and down. That's not going to kill you. At that point you just remember Pat Mesiti saying "If someone spits on me I just get wet. How I react to it is up to me". Don't give them the satisfaction of a reaction. No one can hurt you without your permission. Go back to your table and have a great time.

By now you should have quite a grasp on how to work with attracting what you want by "Tuning In" to your Soul to help you achieve your goals and dreams. Make sure that you expect the good that you desire. The next step is to nurture your Body, Mind and Soul. What you feed grows. Nurturing yourself is not an indulgence it is a necessity. If you take the time to nurture your Body, Mind and Soul you will become more "In Tune" with yourself which will enable you to attract anything you desire in life.

Sometimes moving slower helps to move faster.

Plant the seed of desire in your mind and it forms a nucleus, with power to attract to itself everything needed for it's fulfillment.

- Robert Collier

Part 3
Nurturing Me

Chapter 15

My Time

Doest thou love life?
Then do not squander
time; for that's the stuff
life is made of.

– Benjamin Franklin

My Time

We are now in the third part of the book which is about nurturing and learning to create synergy between your Body, Mind & Soul so that you can achieve your dreams. Making time to nurture yourself is an important part of the process.

I know that your mind may be playing the questioning game here. "Why is it so important?" and "How do I find time?" yada,yada,yada. That's right. Ask the question back to your Mind and allow it to work with your Soul to find the answers. Ask "How do I make time?" Allow the inspiration to come. The answers are inside you. When you make the time for nurturing yourself you will be more powerful in all areas of your life. You will be able to attract what you desire with more ease.

How do *I* find time?

Making the time to work on you is an easy thing to do, it's also just as easy not to do. Designing a life starts with making some choices, planning the day and being disciplined enough to stay on track. Discipline does not have to be a dirty word. A discipline is doing what you need to do to have what you want to have. That's a good thing.

My Time

If you knew that you were going to the movies to see the 7:15 show you would organise your evening to be there on time. That is the same for anything in life that you place value on or make as a priority in your life.

Take the time to write out what you do on a daily basis to give you something to start with. It may even look a little like this.

1. Push the snooze button on the alarm clock several times
2. Fall out of bed and stumble to the shower
3. Hurry to get some breakfast down
4. Rush out the door
5. Work
6. Get home and wind down
7. Eat dinner (sometimes take away)
8. Watch TV
9. Go to bed
10. Wake up the next day to the same thing wondering why you are tired

Look at a typical day for you and see where you could create a space for 15 - 30 minutes a day to begin working on you. That is all you need to start with.

Say no to the good to make way for the great.

My Time

When you say no to the good it means that you may give up a little TV in the evening or a little sleep in the morning, to make way for the great. The great is the feeling or results that you will get for setting that time aside to work on you. With a few little changes you will be surprised what you can fit into your "Me Time".

At the Sleep Institute of England Dr. Jim Horne did an interesting study into the amount of sleep the average person actually requires. The result of the study showed that the average adult only requires 5 and a half to 6 hours sleep. Hmm. Maybe that is a new belief that you can work at creating.

I found that when I suffered with depression I spent a lot of time on the couch or in bed tired. Being depressed took up a lot of energy and time. I wanted to have my life back. If you suffer with depression you may find that forcing yourself to do what I am suggesting may cause you to feel fantastic. All you have to do is choose.

I call it *Me Time*. Once you make the time (like the date at the movies) you plan everything else around it. There are 1440 minutes in a day and what you don't use you lose. I have *Me Time* between 6am and 7am in the morning. It is best for me in the morning because my family is still asleep, the house is quiet and there are no interruptions.

My Time

I remember when I first made the commitment to myself that I would get up earlier. My brain had all sorts of things flying round; it was like a mental tennis match. I set my alarm for 6am. The first morning I said to myself "tomorrow, I'm too tired". I spent the day giving myself a hard time. The next day I hit the snooze button and gave myself an extra 10 minutes and then I got out of bed and put on an Anthony Robbins tape and fell asleep listening to it. (At least I got up) I thought "This is ridiculous".

On the 3rd morning I got up straight away and began to read. It was the best morning that I had had in a long time. At 7am I put the book down and went into the shower feeling great. While I was in the shower all sorts of ideas came into my head. I made a mental note of all of the things I wanted to achieve for the day so that when I was dressed I could write them down. At 7:30am I woke up my husband and children. While they showered I got their lunches and breakfast ready humming to myself. To cut a long story short, I got them to kinder and school early without any arguments, the whole day seemed to go like clock work. I even achieved everything on my "to do list". From that day on I made a habit of getting up at 6am.

I did make the mistake of rolling over one morning and deciding to take the morning off. BIG mistake!

I overslept, ran around like a mad woman yelling at the kids to hurry up. My whole day seemed to be turned upside down by a dumb decision; however it was a great lesson. Not only was I not responsible for me, by beginning my day badly, I gave my children a bad start to the day too.

By adding a little structure to my day it allowed a whole lot more freedom in my life. By doing this over a period of 30 days I formed a habit. If I don't have *Me Time* in the morning now it feels odd, like I haven't brushed my teeth. The morning may not be the ideal time for you so find what works for you and commit to it.

Commitment to Self

I _____ commit

to *Me Time* for _____ Minutes each day

Starting _____

Signed _____

***I* can take control of *my* time.**

You can not control time. However you can control what you do with your time. Once you have successfully added **Me time** to your day you can begin to add in other things like a course or exercise time. It is great to sit down with your diary and see where you can slot in some extra things you would like to achieve.
Learning to say no is an important part of the process. Your time will be demanded from all sorts of people and areas of your life. It is important to remember who is in control of you and your time. You can't always control what happens, however, you can control how you react. It is wiser to stop, re-focus and decide what you are going to do about it.

A good question to ask yourself to help you re-focus and make decisions is . . .

Is this going to take *me* where I want to go?

It is now time to learn about nurturing your Body, Mind and Soul so that you can use your "Me time" effectively to create the results that you want in your life.

Do the thing
and you will get
the energy to do
the thing.

Chapter 16

Nurturing my Body

Nurturing my Body

Looking after our Body is very important. It is no good planning all of the wonderful things to achieve in your life if you are too sick or tired to enjoy them. Some people spend a lot of time and money looking after their car and pay no attention to their Body.

A good diet is a great way to stay healthy; however, lifestyle doesn't always allow proper habits to be formed. Having balance in life means choosing to take control of your diet too. Take the time to create a regime for yourself if you have to until it feels normal to eat well.

Look at your thought processes around eating well, exercising and looking after your Body. You may need to make some adjustments to some of your beliefs in this area.

Include plenty of fresh fruits and vegetables. Avoid sugars and processed foods wherever possible. The more processing the less beneficial it is for your Body. At least 8 glasses of water a day will help hydrate and flush toxins from the Body. Be sensible with your diet. I believe in moderation. It is when things are over consumed that problems can arise. I hear of so many people having food intolerances. Wheat is a common one. If you take a look at what you eat over the day you may find that you have wheat in every meal that you consume. Go back to the basics and you might find it costs a lot less too. If you don't look after your Body who will? You only get one Body! I highly recommend organic, where possible.

We need over 91 nutrients a day. These are made up of minerals, vitamins, antioxidants, amino acids and essential fatty acids. Take the time to do a little research and you will find just how important it is these days to add supplements to our diet. In June of 2002 the Journal of the American Medical Association stated "Harvard University Doctors now recommend that all adults supplement their diet with vitamins and minerals. This is a result of stress, lifestyle, age, medical history, environmental pollution and diet".

I suffered for most of the first 27 years of my life with chronic asthma and we had always eaten a good diet with very little take-away food. I did a little research and swapped my bathroom products to ones without any harmful ingredients, then I began supplementing with vitamins, minerals and antioxidants and I haven't suffered asthma since. A little knowledge in this area is a good thing. If you give your Body what it needs to perform you will find that ill health will be a thing of the past. Focusing on staying healthy is a great thing and always taking your Body towards the next level of health is even better.

Research the chemicals used in and around your home that may also be making your Body struggle just to stay well. I did some research into the potentially harmful ingredients that are in our bathroom products and cosmetics. I was shocked to find out how harmful a lot of the ingredients used in them were, including ones that cause cancer! Changing our personal care products and changing our household cleaners also made a dramatic change to my family's health.

There are companies around who make a point of marketing safe products and high quality nutrition these days. You will find them if you look. It is a matter of "tuning in" to attract what you need. Let your Soul inspire and guide you to find the right ones for you. Don't be fooled by the "natural" slogan. Poison ivy is natural and so is petroleum, but I wouldn't want it on my face. Marketing can sometimes be misleading so do your homework or find someone who has done it for you. Find a company that has integrity when it comes to looking after your health, and the environment.

Your Body does not end there. There are your teeth, your hair, your nails and your skin. I touched on this when I mentioned getting good quality products and trust me all toothpastes are not equal! Taking care of your Body has a lot to do with the habits and beliefs that you have formed which are linked to your self esteem and the beliefs that you have of yourself.

I have found that having a shower and making myself look nice is a great way to nurture my Body and help me feel great. Exercise does the same thing when it gets the endorphins going which are feel good hormones. You not only nurture your Body to be fit, healthy and strong but you feel better too. It does not have to be a big flash physical work out. It can be as simple as taking a walk. Start with a 15 – 20 minute walk and increase it as you get fitter and stronger. The fresh air and Vitamin D from the sun is also good for your Body. Not too many UV rays so wear sun screen and a hat. This is also nurturing the Body as you are not consciously allowing yourself to cause your Body injury or pain.

It doesn't take a lot to make the small changes. The benefit however can be great. Make one change a week if you have to. Within a year you would have changed 52 things. Changing habits and mind sets is the aim of the game here. It doesn't matter if they are small steps as long as they are steps in a forward direction.

Change is usually for the better.

Chapter 17

Nurturing my Mind

Nurturing my Mind

Spend some time each day to work on your Mind. You may read for 15 – 30 minutes from a personal development book, biography, autobiography or you may choose to watch an interesting documentary and learn something new.

Rather than spend the time reading the paper or listening to the news about all of the bad things, (half of them are none of your business and the other half are depressing), use the time to develop yourself. I'm not saying don't be informed. I am saying that there are a lot of things we don't need to continually keep impressing on the Mind.

Working on me is a large part of my life. **"Take time to practice your craft"** is a belief of mine. It is not just the knowing but putting into practice what I learn. It's called being congruent. If you are shooting for a particular goal wouldn't it make sense to learn more about how to get it?

What would you like to learn? Is it a language, a musical instrument or photography? This is the time in the day that you would use to practice or learn more on a special interest. Fulfilling these needs is a great part of feeling fulfilled.

Nurturing my Mind

Nurturing the Mind can also be time for re-training the Mind. It might be that you have noticed a belief or a habit that you have or something that you want to "program" yourself with. Is this a form of brain washing? Absolutely! You clean your Body every day don't you? So why wouldn't you want to clean your Mind to get rid of some of that "stinkin thinkin".

There are some wonderful techniques for doing this and I have covered some of them earlier in the book. Some people choose to listen to a loop CD overnight while they are sleeping to help with re-programming their mind. This is where you play a CD on a loop cycle while you are sleeping. If you are learning French you may play a French tape. There are some fantastic CDs that have powerful sayings like "I deserve to be happy and have it all". It can be you recording your own voice with all of the great things that you are going to achieve. This is a good one as you trust your own voice.

I do not suggest going to sleep with the television on or the radio. Think for a minute of what is on the television and some of the lyrics on some of the songs and the news flashes. Do you want your Mind to be bombarded and programmed with all of the negative and doom and gloom stuff? Again, I am not saying here not to keep informed of what is going on in the world. I am saying be responsible for what goes into your Mind just like your Body. If you don't, nobody else will.

Nurturing my Mind

Another good way to program your Mind is with a technique called "22 x 11" you can find the technique in the book "Absolute Happiness" written by Michael Domeyko Rowland. Go to your local library or book store and get some more great books to further your knowledge.

You may want to increase your knowledge on the personality types as I suggested earlier in the book. It will all help. Listen to your Soul as it will guide and inspire you to get what you need.

Make sure to program your Mind with the feelings using the different senses as this will be more powerful in forming a belief or habitual way of thinking. Positive chemicals will be sent around the Body and the cells will respond in the way that you would like them to. Audio can be CDs and Visual could be a dream board. Get creative with the process.

Chapter 18
Nurturing my Soul

Nurturing my Soul

Nurturing my Soul is the most fun part of nurturing me. There are so many ways to nurture your Soul and I really encourage you to find as many as you can. I will not give you all of the answers. Not because it would make it too easy for you, but because it is far more rewarding when you figure them out for yourself.

Many people have a misnomer that they have to sit and meditate to be able to connect with their Soul. I believe that there are many exciting ways to nurture the Soul. Meditation is definitely a great way to start. Sitting still and taking the time to still the Mind and connect is a great discipline. It enables you to slow down to move faster.

There are lots of different ways to meditate and "connect". A great one to try is sitting and observing a flower or a blade of grass that is moving or swaying with the breeze. (It is also a fantastic way to connect with nature and the earth.) Sit and watch the blade of grass or flower until there is nothing. No chatter in the Mind, nothing. You may then hear your Soul inspiring you with all sorts of ideas. Meditation takes practice. If you focus too hard, all you will hear is your Mind chattering. Just relax and focus on the blade of grass or flower. Enjoy the process of sitting and letting yourself go to that magical place where your greatest ideas and inspirations lie.

I find my inspiration when I am having a shower. I don't want to give you any visuals, but, the shower is a relaxing way to nurture my Soul. When I stand in the shower with the water running over my face, I become aware that there is nothing. I appear to "go somewhere". Some people would call it day dreaming. This is usually when I get some of my best ideas. I am conscious that I don't spend too long in the shower because of water restrictions. I stay in long enough to feel refreshed and recharged.

Yesterday I was in the shower when I heard my Soul say "take a look at what is happening to you right now". I observed myself singing a catchy tune while I was dancing and tapping my side. I also became aware that while I was doing this I was thinking of ideas for my book. This insight was one of them. Next time you take a shower you could try it out for yourself. Relax, let the water run over your face and let your Mind go blank then see what inspiration comes.

Aboriginals and most native cultures connect to their "spirits" while they sing, dance, clap, chant, and play instruments.

My husband (Paul is very creative and good with his hands) has noticed that when he is in his garage enjoying making something he gets some of his best ideas. This also happens for him when he is out in the bush riding his motorbike.

Nurturing my Soul

I believe that anything you enjoy, where you can switch off from your Mind and problems and get "lost in your thoughts" to the point where great ideas pop into your head, you are nurturing and connecting with your Soul. It may be floating in a pool on an air bed, scrap booking or walking the dog. You may want to keep a pen and paper handy to write down any ideas or inspiration that you have. Write down your idea then continue with what you were doing.

If your Mind wanders to a "negative thought," consciously think of something positive (you may wish to use an affirmation) then allow your Mind to go blank and become immersed in the creative process.

Make nurturing your Soul fun. Enjoy the connection and inspiration that it brings. Connect with your feelings. Dance, sing and don't worry what anyone thinks. What a great way to clean the house!

Part 4
Creating Magic

Chapter 19

Where am I going?

Where am I going?

I have taken you on a journey into who you are, how to work with your Body, Mind and Soul and how to nurture yourself. You have the tools to work with the powerful person that you are. Whether you believe it or not you are already a winner. (You beat all of the other sperm to the egg.) Now, by reading this book, you are taking the steps to enable you to achieve everything you put your Mind and Soul to.

So where do you want to go? What do you want to do?

If you are not sure at this point, it's okay. When I began to think about what I wanted, I didn't know what it was. I had somewhere along the line lost my ability to dream. I started thinking "What am I supposed to do with my life?" I didn't have all of the information that you have now back when I began my journey. I put myself under pressure trying to force the answers and shut my filter down which took me further away from being able to hear my Soul speak. I believed that I had to have it all figured out, then, I started to relax and take the pressure off myself by saying "I don't have to know that yet but I'll know it when I get there. Until then I'll just keep moving forward and working on improving and getting to know myself, my Mind and my Soul"

There are some people who just seem to know what

they want to do and have it all figured out. There is no point giving yourself a hard time or being envious over it. As you know that will only push what you want further away by shutting down the creative process. Find a space where you can connect with your Soul and ask some simple questions. The solutions are usually simple as you have probably already noticed.

SO what do *you* want?

At this stage, you may not know what it is but let's explore what it could be like if you did know. Explore these points when you answer the questions and beware of the Mind.

- What would it be?
- What would it look like?
- How would it make *me* feel?

Spend some time answering these questions. It is important to note how it makes you feel. If it makes you feel good then you know you are on track. If it doesn't make you feel good then it may be that you do it out of obligation or because you think that that is what you are meant to do.

These answers are for you and you alone. Remember it is about you.

Where am I going?

1. What do *I* spend *my* time thinking about?

   _____

   _____

2. What do *I* visualise?

   _____

   _____

3. What do *I* tend to spend *my* money on? (exclude bills)

   _____

   _____

4. What is important to *me*?

   _____

   _____

5. What do *I* love to do?

   _____

   _____

Where am I going?

6. What do *I* find myself drawn to talk about?

_____

_____

7. What do I fill *my* surroundings with?

_____

_____

8. What makes *me* really excited or angry?

_____

_____

9. What gives *me* the feeling of satisfaction?

_____

_____

10. Where am *I* organised or disciplined?

_____

_____

11. What achievements have I made that have made me feel really good?

_____

_____

_____

_____

Now go and ask your family and friends about the answers that you came up with. They may say "Yeah, that really gets you revved up" or "No, I think you are more passionate about . . ." This will give you some clues as to how other people see you.

What are the clues that you have learnt about yourself that you are passionate about being, doing or having in your life?

What I love and value highly in my life is . . .

_____

_____

_____

_____

Where am I going?

I had been learning about myself for quite a number of years when something compelled me to want to write. I would read in the morning and get the urge to write down the things that I had put together for myself. I knew that what I was writing was for me to learn and master for myself then, one day, the thought came to me that if I published a book containing the information that I had learnt that had helped me, it could also help millions of people.

I then caught myself thinking "Why would anyone read my book? I'm no personal development guru". After thinking about it for a long time and keeping my thoughts to myself, I discussed it with a friend who thought it was a great idea. After all, I had already been verbally sharing what I know with others and had empowered them to make changes in their lives. I began to see myself on stage teaching what I now know to large groups of people and became very excited at the thought of empowering others to take control of their lives. There was a big key there when I began to feel excited. The more I discussed it the more others encouraged me. I didn't have to be a guru. I thought to myself "I wouldn't be having these visions if I couldn't do it; and there are millions of people out there who could use this information so who am I to keep it to myself. I am robbing them of all of these great insights" Here I am today talking to you, doing what I value and love, which fulfills me. I feel like I am connected to you with my Soul and it feels fantastic to be able to help you in creating the life that you deserve to have.

The same can be for you. Find what it is that you love and value. Use the clues that you have just discovered for yourself and in the next chapter I will help you to create a bigger picture so that you can put in the necessary steps to achieve your dreams. This is not a practice run. You only get one shot at this lifetime so why not make it a good one?

> "If you go to work on your goals, your goals will go to work on you.
> If you go to work on your plan, your plan will go to work on you.
> Whatever good things we build end up building us."
>
> - Jim Rohn

Chapter 20

My Plan

You will never change your life until you change something you do daily. The secret of your success is found in your daily routine.

– John C. Maxwell

My Plan

By completing the exercises throughout the book you will probably have begun changes in your life and have chosen a new direction. You may have been inspired to do some new things that you may never have thought possible before. It is now time to create a plan of action.

It is not much good putting a plan into place to change the actions if you do not change the thoughts behind the belief. Be conscious of your thoughts and feelings while you are completing these exercises as you may need to make some mental adjustments on the way.

Allowing yourself to be who you are, living in line with what you value and working with your Soul to attract what you want is very powerful. Now that you have a fairly good idea of where you want to go you can put into place the baby steps in order to achieve your goals.

Happiness is found within.

Creating a Daily Plan

The first step is to free up some time by creating a little discipline in your everyday life. Having a little structure in your day allows more flexibility to add in the exciting steps to achieve your goals. It may involve saying no to

My Plan

the "good" to make way for the "great" as discussed in the chapter My Time. If necessary, review the chapter to help give you more clarity.

In the space below, fill in a rough estimate of what you would like to have in your day, make sure to include what you value and time to nurture the whole self. State the time that you intend to wake and a rough estimate of what time you will go to bed. I understand that each day will be different depending on your commitments. Write down the things that you want in your day that are not negotiable.

_____

_____

_____

_____

_____

_____

_____

_____

_____

My Plan

Begin with a Yearly Plan

The next step is to work out what your goals are for the next 12 months. When you have established clear goals the steps can be broken down into half year, monthly and weekly steps to achieve all of your goals.

Write down the 8 goals that you intend to achieve in the next 12 months. Ideally to create balance in your life you would have one from each of these areas: personal, relationships, career/business, physical, financial, time out, contribution and spiritual. However, this is your plan so choose the goals that are in line with what you love and value. Write down the area, the goal and the reason you would like to achieve that goal.

Example   **Play squash**   **To be fit, energetic**
                      3 times a week   **and healthy**

	Goal	Reason
1		
2		

My Plan

	Goal	Reason
3		
4		
5		
6		
7		
8		

You should have 8 goals that you wish to accomplish in the next 12 months. Some of these goals may be completed within the first month, some in 6 months and so on. There may be more goals that you would like to add to your plan. To stretch yourself add 2 more goals.

	Goal	Reason
9		
10		

Now you have your ten goals to achieve in the next 12 months. This is an exciting time. You may be looking at them with excitement and be itching to get stuck into achieving them. You may be looking at them all and feel a little scared at the thought of how you are going to fit them all into your life. The excited but scared feeling is a great place to be as you are hearing and connecting to both your Mind & your Soul. No matter where you are take a deep breath, relax and work with your Mind & Soul to plan how you will achieve them. Have a staggered start to each of your goals. You may start something new each month.

If you start with one goal and achieve it you will feel great and then you can move on to the next goal. This will be easier than trying to fit in ten new things and end up feeling overwhelmed and quit on some, if not all, of them. Over a period of five years you could end up achieving 50 new goals. Exciting when you see it like this isn't it?

Rate the ten goals in order of which month you would like to begin.

1._____

2._____

3._____

My Plan

4._____

5._____

6._____

7._____

8._____

9._____

10._____

With your list of ten goals in order you are ready to begin. Create a rough plan as to how you intend to achieve each of the goals. Let's begin with an example . . .

Belly dancing classes.

June – find out costs of the course and any special clothing that needs to purchased.

July & August – save up for course and clothing.

September – enroll and begin classes.

December – show the family how well I am doing in the end of year concert.

My Plan

Take the ten goals and begin filling out a **Half Year Plan**. Work out what you will need to have completed to be on track for achieving your goals by the end of the year. Some of your goals may require preparation time.

Once you have completed the Half Year plan. Break down the steps for the **Monthly Plan** in the same way. You may need to complete a new plan for each month. Looking over your plan at the end of the month using and regrouping yourself (which I will show you how in the next chapter) will help you in completing your plan for the following month.

Once you have broken down what you will be required to do each month use the **Weekly Plan** to break down the steps further. Complete as many weekly Plans as required. You may require only one sheet as there may be only one step to fill in for each goal and you can refer to the same sheet for all of the goals individually in the month that you require it. Use your diary, phone or organiser to place reminders of tasks that need to be completed. This way you will keep your Mind free in the knowledge that you won't forget anything that requires to be done.

To achieve your goals it may be useful to find mentors and coaches who will help and encourage you. A mentor will encourage and support you while a coach who has the knowledge will train you in the necessary skills that you require to succeed.

My Plan

A daily, weekly, monthly, half yearly and yearly regrouping will help you to see if you are on track, or if your goals have changed or are no longer a focus. When challenges arise you have the knowledge to know that you can find all of the answers. Your mentors and coaches will also be able to guide and encourage you to move forward in the direction of your goals.

Half Year Plan

What do I have to do, be, have or have completed to be on track for each goal at the half year mark?

1. _____

   _____

2. _____

   _____

3. _____

   _____

4. _____

   _____

My Plan

5. _____

_____

6. _____

_____

7. _____

_____

8. _____

_____

9. _____

_____

10. _____

_____

Notes, comments, concerns or need to investigate

Monthly Plan Month _____

What do I have to do, be, have or have completed to be on track for each goal this month?

1. _____

_____

2. _____

_____

3. _____

_____

4. _____

_____

5. _____

_____

6. _____

_____

My Plan

7. _____

_____

8. _____

_____

9. _____

_____

10. _____

_____

Notes, comments, concerns or need to investigate

My Plan

Weekly Plan Week Ending _____

What do *I* have to do, be, have or have completed to be on track for each goal this week?

1. _____

_____

2. _____

_____

3. _____

_____

4. _____

_____

5. _____

_____

6. _____

_____

My Plan

7._____

_____

8._____

_____

9._____

_____

10._____

_____

Notes, comments, concerns or need to investigate

Chapter 21

Regrouping Diary

Regrouping Diary

Daily Regrouping

The daily regrouping is a great way to finish the day in a positive mood and by setting the vibration for the following day, your sleep should be much more restful.

Regrouping is a positive exercise which allows you to see all of the great things that you have created in your life for the day. It also gives you time to reflect on all of the people and things that you are grateful for having in your life. When I say "things" it may mean inspiration or quality traits that you have. Happiness starts from the inside, not from material possessions. Taking time to be grateful for what you have is a powerful process which will connect you to your Soul. If your day has been a little negative you may choose to pick up the diary and read from past days. This can inspire you with the knowledge that you can create great things. By focusing on all of the positive achievements that you make you will be drawn to create more of the same and better.

Use the following questions as a guide or obtain a copy from the website to photocopy and use each day. You may want to purchase a **Daily Regrouping Diary** which has these questions in it. It is set out to inspire you with lots of great words of wisdom for further insight.

I hope you enjoy the revelations each day as much as I enjoy regrouping my day.

Once you have completed your daily regrouping it is great to think about what you are going to achieve in the following day. Take the time to write a **"to do list"** for the following day. As you sleep you may come up with ideas of how to effortlessly achieve some of the items on your list setting you up for a powerful day ahead.

Remember, if the day didn't go as planned that's ok.
What insights did you get from the day?
Re-set yourself for the next day as it is a fresh start.
Remain positive and keep your positive feelings connected towards your goal.

Peace comes from within. Don't seek it without.

– Buddah

My Daily Regrouping for

_____ 20____

Who/what am *I* grateful for having in *my* life today?

_____

_____

What did *I* give of *myself* to someone today? How did it make *me* feel? (compliment, smile, encouragement etc)

_____

_____

What did *I* notice that *I* attracted today?

_____

_____

What did *I* read/listen to that was inspiring today?

_____

_____

Regrouping Diary

What action did *I* take to achieve my goals and dreams today?

_____

_____

What was the highlight of *my* day?

_____

_____

Did *I* honor myself with *Me Time*?

_____

_____

What did *I* learn during *Me Time* that will support *me* in achieving my goals and dreams?

_____

_____

Did *I* learn anything new today?

_____

_____

Notes . . .

My Weekly Regrouping for

_____ 20____

What did *I* do towards *my* goals and dreams this week?

_____

_____

Are there any questions or concerns *I* need to address?

_____

_____

What could *I* do differently to improve *my* results?

_____

_____

What was the highlight of *my* week?

_____

_____

Am *I* on track to achieve *my* goals?

_____

_____

Regrouping Diary

How do *I* feel about *my* goals now?

_____

_____

Are *my* goals still in line with where *I* am going?

_____

_____

Are there any goals *I* need to amend, delete or add?

_____

_____

Did *I* honor *myself* with enough *Me Time* this week?

_____

What did *I* learn during *Me Time* that will support *me* to achieve *my* goals and dreams?

_____

_____

Notes . . .

My Monthly Regrouping for

_____ **20**____

What did *I* do towards *my* goals and dreams this month that had a positive result?

_____

_____

_____

Are there any questions or concerns *I* need to address?

_____

_____

_____

What can *I* do differently to improve *my* results?

_____

_____

What was the highlight of *my* month?

_____

_____

Regrouping Diary

Am *I* on track to achieve *my* goals?

_____

_____

Who/what am *I* grateful for in *my* life this month?

_____

_____

Are there any goals *I* need to amend, delete or add?

_____

_____

_____

What did *I* learn about *myself* this month that has made a positive change in *my* life? How does it make *me* feel?

_____

_____

Notes . . .

Chapter 22

Me Sharing

Me Sharing

Now that you are excited with the results you are getting in your life it is natural that you will talk to people about what you have learnt. It is important to be aware that not everyone is in the same space that you are in now. Some may notice the change in you and not know how to deal with the new you and others may be inspired by the new you. Realise that the ones who don't know how to deal with you are reacting because they may not understand or have not adjusted to the new you yet, give them time. Some may not want to understand and that is okay too. You are only responsible for you.

How do I share?

Empowering others to take charge of their life and create can be very exciting. I get a big buzz out of it. I remember when I began my journey I was so excited; I wanted to tell everyone so that they could also experience this great feeling. The trouble was that some of them were not ready to hear about it and they probably felt that I was pushing my views onto them as I was saying things like "You should read this book . . . it would be good for you". "Should, huh!" they probably thought.

The best way to share with others is to lead by example. No one really likes to be told that what they are doing is short of what they could achieve, so I continued working on me. Then when others would ask me what I was doing I would share what worked for me and say things like "I read this great book and it really helped me to realise things about myself and showed me simple ways to make changes". If they asked what the book was I offered to lend it to them or told them where they could get hold of a copy. It is really important not to try to, as they say, "dump the truck load" on them. This is where you give them a full rundown on the book. If you do that they can feel overwhelmed as well as giving them no reason to go out and read it for themselves.

It is natural that we don't want the people who we love and care about to go through the same challenges that we have. I know that when I was younger my Mother and Father would warn me off doing something and I sometimes did it anyway, this was because I had to learn the lesson for myself. If I hadn't made those mistakes then I wouldn't have learnt other things either. We can guide others by making suggestions and they will then choose to accept them or not. People don't like to be made to be wrong, they love it when they feel empowered enough to make decisions that they feel good about.

Empower rather than help.

Me Sharing

When I began my journey I realised that I liked to help people. In the process of helping people I would wonder why they were not taking responsibility for themselves and began to rely on me for the solutions to their problems. What a heavy burden that was to take on other people's problems as well as working through my own stuff. As time went by I began to realise the difference between helping someone and empowering someone. By helping someone I take away their responsibility and make them weak. Empowering someone gives them strength.

Have patience with others and have patience with yourself. Remember it is a journey, not a destination. Enjoy the journey. Remember not to look back at the negative things. Know where you are going using your knowledge and guidance. Be careful not to live in the future, but stay in the now. That's why they call it the "present" as it is a gift.

Enjoy the process of your metamorphosis. Use and share your skills to create an exciting adventure during this experience that you are having.

Empowering others is an important step of sharing. Whilst having coffee with someone I had known for a while, he asked me what book I would suggest for him to figure out a certain area of his life. We happened to be near a Borders store at the time so I suggested that we take a wander over to the self help section. When we got there he started looking at one side and I began looking at the other. I looked at lots of books and actually found a couple for myself when all of a sudden he said "You won't believe it". He picked up a book which had almost the identical title which he said that he was struggling with. It was displayed with the cover facing forward rather than the spine facing out.

I was excited for him. Later I shared with him that if I had found a book for him on the subject he would continue to come to me for the answers or might not take the information as seriously as if he had found it himself. If I had told him to go to Borders so that he would find a book himself that would be just what he needed he might have looked so hard that he may have been caught in his Mind and missed what he was looking for. He may not have gone at all. Using the law of Attraction to "Tune In" and me "holding his hand" he was open to inspiration and was able to see the book he needed out of all the other books on display. Now he is empowered enough to know that when he needs answers he can go and find them. It is still okay to ask but ensure that the person whom you are asking is getting results in the area you are asking about. What a great feeling for him because he found it and also for myself having the opportunity to share in the process.

Who do I share with?

There will be people in life who love and care about

you and don't want to see you "hurt". I have seen people share their dreams with others only to have them squashed and be ridiculed for thinking that they could achieve their dream. This can be very damaging to someone who is beginning their journey.

Before taking someone's advice look at the results that they are getting in that area of their life. Are they qualified to give you advice? Everyone has an opinion; it doesn't mean that you have to agree with it. You probably wouldn't ask a plumber for electrical advice. Make sure you are getting the right advice not just an opinion. Smile, say thank you for the advice then make your own choice or seek the advice you need elsewhere to make the right choice for you.

Sometimes there are the ones who are jealous of where you are at, they see what you have and secretly want it. They may not recognise this consciously and may ridicule you to make them feel better for where they are at. It is like crabs in a bucket.

If you go crabbing and put one crab in a bucket it will try to get out. If you place more than one crab in the bucket and watch, when one tries to climb out the others pull it back down. I'm not sure if it is the "misery loves company" or if they are pulling the other one down to climb on top of it to get themselves out. It is worth identifying if it happens to you and realise it for what it is. Naturally we all want people to do well in life

and it will not be a direct reflection on you, it is just an indication of how they feel about where they are at.
If you have a dream that is big and bold be selective on whom you share your dreams with. Find yourself a few people that you know will support you to achieve your goals and dreams until you feel strong enough to tell the world. You will know who they are. If you do happen to share with someone that you shouldn't, you have the strategies to choose the way that you feel so that you can remain on track.

Surround yourself with like minded people who will support and encourage you. Distance yourself from "toxic" relationships. As they say "don't go as often and don't stay as long". Sometimes they may move away from you. Don't be hurt as sometimes there are reasons and seasons for each relationship. Some people come into our life just for a short time; value the relationship for what it was. Be grateful and move on.

Mutual sharing

You may find that once you have begun your journey, you will attract others into your life that have begun their own journey. When you have others that are journeying as you are, you are able to support each other. It may not be the same journey as we are all different. What I need to learn and what you need to learn from a book may be vastly different. Sharing those differences may help both of you to learn something on a deeper level that you may not have thought of on your own. Different beliefs may give a different perspective.

It is great to have a discussion or form a group. Each person can share what they have put together. This is exciting as there is no right and wrong. You will always get what you need at the time. By having someone else share from their eyes they may give a whole new perspective again. It is important not to judge others or yourself as it is all part of the learning process depending on where you are on your journey. By taking the suggested use of this book at the beginning and sharing together you may all learn and support each other at the same time. Encourage and help each other to stay accountable for taking the steps required to achieve your goals.

> Give a man a fish,
> feed him for a day.
> Teach a man to fish,
> feed him for a lifetime.

Chapter 23

My Patience

My Patience

This chapter is like a little innoculation (injection) before you begin putting your plans into action. It is to protect you from disappointment in the times when you feel things are not happening as fast as you would like them to.

Sowing and reaping

There are four seasons in a year. In Australia we call them Summer, Autumn, Winter and Spring. Each season brings different weather and conditions.

We need to prepare for each season. A squirrel will collect and store nuts for the winter. Humans may collect fire wood to keep warm for the winter and clear the fire debris for summer when the fire season is nearing.

The same for the farmer. There is a season (time) when he has to prepare the ground, there is a season to plant his crop, a season when he has to tend and water the crop and finally comes the season to harvest the crop. Quite often the ground is allowed to rest before the next season begins.

In the preparing and planting of the crop there is a

lot of work to be done. While the crop is growing the work load is not as great because nature does most of the work. Harvesting can be a very busy time and then the farmer gets to reap the rewards after the harvest is complete.

There are times in our life when we need to put in the required work or actions to get the result that we want and there are times when we reap the rewards.

When you are working a job they do not put money in your pocket constantly throughout the day. You work the amount of time whether it is a week, a fortnight or a month and then you get paid. Each day a student studies they don't have an indication of where their examination results will be. They have to wait until the exams are marked after the year of learning and studying.

It is important to remember that there is a time for sowing (action) and a time for reaping (reward) but they don't happen at the same time.

Timing in nature

In nature we can time things. With animals we call it a gestation time and with plants we call it a growing time before harvest.

Gestation times vary between different animals. A dog is approximately 9 weeks, horses 340 days, elephants 22 months and humans are 40 weeks or approximately 9 months.

Growing times of vegetables are usually shorter. Spring onions are 25 – 30 days, peas are 45 – 60 days, potatoes take 90 days to full maturity and carrots can range from 120 – 150 days to harvest.

The farmer does not go out into the field during the growing season and pull it up to see if it is growing because he understands that things take time. Women don't hang around waiting to go into labor from the 6th month because they know it is not time for the baby to come yet.

Nature is easy to predict but when we don't have a time frame to work with I understand that we can get a little impatient.

Timing of goals

Let me now give you a better understanding of timing. It is the timing for achieving a goal.

Remember earlier in the book I said that things may vibrate at different speeds. I used water as an example. If you slow down the vibration of the water by freezing

it then it becomes ice. If you heat the water you speed up the vibration and it becomes steam. If you heat it and speed it up further it becomes air, ether or gas.
The more physical or dense the object is; the vibration (or state) is usually slower. The faster the vibration of the object the less we can see it with the naked eye. Air is a great example of how fast it can move. By blowing the air we can move it away quite quickly and power a paper boat across water.

You may wonder how this applies to the timing of your goals. When you set a goal you put the Body, Mind and Soul to work. You start attracting or repelling what you need. I am going to use an analogy to help you understand what happens when we get impatient or doubt.

If things move faster in the unseen time then it may come quite quickly just like the wind. If it doesn't happen when you thought that it might you could begin to doubt or become impatient. This will shut down the attraction process which is like blowing the wind in the opposite direction. If you re-focus you will draw the air back towards you again. You may continue to repeat this process for a while. It would be like taking two steps forward and one step back. You will eventually get to your destination but it takes more time and energy than was actually required.

It is wiser to set up a time period to achieve the goal,

continue to put the necessary steps in place and you will achieve it.

Staying on track

Sometimes when you are on the journey towards a goal and you are in the action stage and the results are not showing yet, this understanding will help to keep you on track.

It would be like being on a train to Perth from Melbourne. You would see desert for a long while with no sight of Perth but you know that the train is on the right track and you will get there in due time. What you see around you is not always a true indication to where you are going but it is part of the journey towards the destination.

There is not much difference between the train ride and reaching your goals. If you have a plan in place and follow the actions and steps required towards reaching your goal you will get there. It is important to work with the Body, Mind and Soul. If you stay relaxed and open then the ideas and inspiration that you need will come. You will be attracting everything that you need to be successful. Have patience and your rewards will come sooner than you expect.

Slow down to move faster.

Affirmations

An affirmation is a sentence that you repeat over and over throughout the day to affirm what you want to have in your life. It can be about material things or character traits that you are wanting to develop in yourself or a goal that you want to achieve.

Affirmations are a fantastic way to stay focused when you are in the action stage as they help to keep you on track. They will form the habits and beliefs in the Mind which affirm the feeling that goes along with the goal and the Body will then take the required action.

There are some important things to keep in mind when you are writing affirmations.

By now you should have a good grasp on how the Body, Mind and Soul functions. Affirmations work with the processes of the Body, Mind and Soul and can work quickly to "program" the belief or habit that you need to have.

Keep it in the present tense – If you "want to have" something then act as if you have it. If you have it as something in the future you will get what you want and it will always be in the future. If you want to achieve it now or be in the process of achieving it now then make sure that it is in the now.

Make it believable and empowering – It is important to work with the feeling that the affirmation creates. You want the type of chemical that will be sent around the Body to be the right one. If you have an affirmation that says "I am slim and fit" and you are a large person then when you say the affirmation your Mind may be saying "Oh yeah you still look fat to me" then the Brain will send a chemical around the Body which gives you a bad feeling. If you notice that your thoughts are not in line then you are being counter reactive and both will cancel each other out with a neutral response.

To make it believable you may say something like "I am in the process of becoming slim and fit". What the Mind will do then is say "yeah" and think of all of the things that you are currently doing towards reaching that goal which will affirm the statement and send good messages and feelings around the Body.

Keep it short, concise and on one topic – If you use too many words you will lose the impact of the statement. By putting more than one topic in the statement you may also send confusing or conflicting messages to the Mind. It is okay to be saying many affirmations throughout your day as long as you make each one a separate statement which states what you want to affirm.

You could have a separate affirmation for every goal that you wish to set. You may not need to do this if one big goal will help you to achieve the little goals on the way. It is your choice as it is your journey.

Use affirmations as often as you like. Repetition is the key to forming the habits and beliefs in your Mind. You can say them out loud (people may look at you strangely in public though) or in your Mind. You can memorise them and repeat them to yourself throughout the day or read them to yourself from a goal card which could be a reminder in your wallet, purse or pocket.

Another effective way to use your affirmations is to record them in your own voice and listen to them over night on a loop play. You could also try saying them to yourself while you are looking into a mirror. This method may really challenge you by bringing up other emotions and beliefs about yourself; however, it is very powerful and will help you to work on other areas of your growth.

Now you have all the tools to confidently get started lets move on to the beginning of your new journey…

All great achievements require time.

- Maya Angelou

Part 5
The Beginning

Chapter 24

The Beginning

Whatever you can
do or dream,
you can begin it,
boldness has
genius, power
and magic in it.

– Goethe

The Beginning

In the Introduction I said that the end was really the beginning. You have begun a journey that can take you wherever you choose to go. You really can create magic.

By having a clear understanding of who you are, and the knowledge that your thoughts, feelings and actions create the results in your life, you can create any result you put your Mind and Soul to. The exercises that I have given you can be used in all areas of your life.

By setting a Plan, Regrouping and having gratitude you can monitor your thoughts and alter your course. All it takes is beginning. Beginning takes boldness. Begin it now.

Take the time to dream. It doesn't matter how big the goal is you can break it down into bite size pieces. Dream big. What do you really want in life? What do you really want to achieve? Who do you want to be?

Write down exactly what you want your life to be like 2 years from now, 5 years from now and 10 years from now.

The Beginning

The Beginning

_____

_____

_____

_____

_____

_____

_____

_____

_____

_____

_____

_____

Follow your dreams and share your successes. Go out and achieve all that your heart desires. Give, laugh and love while having gratitude for the life you create. You deserve it.

There is magic,
but you have to be
the magician.
You have to make
the magic happen.

- Sidney Sheldon

Final Note

I warmly congratulate you for working through this book. If you have completed all of the exercises you have all the skills to create a wonderful life that is rich with potential.

Continue to study these concepts, planning and acting on your goals and you shall have success year after year beyond your wildest dreams. Pick up new books, learn new concepts and fall in love with making a difference in your life. Shine and you will be a beacon of hope for others.

Connecting with you has been a pleasure. I hope that my sharing has allowed you to find the wonder in *you* and given you the belief that you really can create magic in your own life. Follow your dreams and I look forward to connecting with you again.

Be the change
you wish to see
in the world.

- Mahatma Gandhi

Dedication

I dedicate this book to my
wonderful husband Paul
and our two amazing children
Matthew and Joel.

You inspire me to do more, be more and
have more so in turn I may give more.

Thank you

My heart felt thanks to all of the people who have
supported, encouraged and helped during the
creation of this book. You know who you are
and I am sincerely blessed to have you in my life.
Extra special thanks to Leonor Ramage
and Fran Boon for your insights and inspiration.

I thank you, the reader, for taking the time to
connect and allowing me to take you on a journey.
This is just the beginning . . .

Create Magic and keep
the Wonder in You Alive

www.ingramcontent.com/pod-product-compliance
Lightning Source LLC
Chambersburg PA
CBHW071702160426
43195CB00012B/1549